MARX & ENGELS ON LITERATURE & ART

MARX & ENGELS ON LITERATURE & ART

a selection of writings

edited by Lee Baxandall & Stefan Morawski
introduction by Stefan Morawski

Telos Press, St. Louis/Milwaukee

The editors wish to acknowledge a generous grant from the Louis M. Rabinowitz Foundation which helped make this volume possible. An earlier version of the introductory essay appeared in the *Journal of Aesthetics and Art Criticism*.

ISBN: 0-914386-02-6 (paper edition)
0-914386-01-8 (hard cover edition)

Library of Congress Catalog Card Number: 73-93501

Manufactured in the United States of America.

TABLE OF CONTENTS

MARX & ENGELS
ON LITERATURE & ART

The selection and ordering of the texts which follow depart from the practice of earlier editors.

Dialectical and historical materialism is the context in which the aesthetic thought is cradled and in which it functions. And yet, we have included relatively few basic philosophical statements by Marx and Engels. We found it unnecessary to extend the book or to encumber the aesthetic texts by making reference to fundamental writings which are not only easily obtainable elsewhere but can be better presented and understood in their complete context. Of course, we have benefitted a great deal from the pioneering editions by Mikhail Lifshitz. Even here, the reader will surely understand that we thought to improve on earlier approaches.

Accordingly, what choices and dispositions of texts were made? Included is the basic aesthetic thought of Marx and Engels. The selections deal in part with the allogenetic aspects (the external relations) of art, and they bear partly on the idiogenetic aspects of art (its relative autonomy and specificity). Because the latter aspects have generally been neglected or pushed into the background, we have taken care to provide an adequate representation of this side of Marxian aesthetic thought.

The basic texts are patterned around what are discerned as the dominant themes of Marx and Engels in this area. To these dominant themes, some less developed observations and remarks may be attached. See Section II of the introductory essay for an explanation of this practice. We stress that no attempt has been made to give an exhaustive documentation; if the reader seeks added reading in the less basic or more peripheral texts bearing on the arts (e.g., incidental remarks on writers or artists, whether or not in the context of the dominant themes), the most recent German or Russian language collections should be consulted. Section III of the introductory essay offers a general methodological perspective of the dominant themes. To more fully grasp the Marxian world view one should read the philosophical works of Marx and Engels and also those of their most authentic interpreters, e.g., Lenin, Gramsci, Lukács.

In further structuring the material we would have liked to observe two criteria: an order of documents within each dominant thematic area according to the dates of their writing, and an arrangement of the material for each theme which would move from general to progressively more particular applications. Obviously, both aims could not be simultaneously accomplished. We had to choose, and we organized each of the dominant themes so that the texts might be read according to the date of composition. As a result, the concrete historical analysis of an issue will sometimes precede the general statements by Marx and Engels (this is especially so for alienation). Perhaps it should be explicitly pointed out that the section headings are only suggestive of emphasis—they are not intended to limit the scope of the material or to provide a hard-and-fast definition. When writing on history, ideology, and art, Marx and Engels usually discuss several matters which are pertinent to this book and included in a single text. For example, alienation and class values are surely inseparable; but in order to emphasize the central role played by alienation in the aesthetic thought of Marx and Engels, it is distinguished here from other themes. For another reason we have introduced the texts on Lamartine, a poet, as a specifically political figure. It seemed important to avoid giving the impression that Marx and Engels wrote about the works of poets without regard for the character of their lives; and indeed, the latter kind of text is as frequent as the former. However, we believe that the approach where one looks first to the artistic product of an artistic worker (e.g., the treatment of Chateaubriand) is not only more central to the Marxian heritage but has more obvious relevance for the student of aesthetic thought. Our general approach has also led us to present a number of texts in part rather than in whole. Ellipses indicate where internal passages are omitted, and brackets enclose a few brief editorial emendations to texts. Explanatory notes are provided where necessary.

INTRODUCTION

I. *A Note on the Texts and Previous Interpretations*

A fairly extensive literature of interpretations of the aesthetic thought of Karl Marx (1818-1883) already exists. The bibliography of writings on the aesthetic thought of Frederick Engels (1820-1895) is rather smaller. To begin with, the relevant surviving texts of Marx and Engels were collected for the first time in Russian in the early Thirties (*Ob iskusstvje*, ed. Anatoli Lunacharsky, Mikhail Lifshitz, and Franz P. Schiller [Moscow, 1933]). Indeed, many important manuscripts had turned up but a few years previously. This volume signalled the beginning of an adequate attention from scholars and a growing measure of recognition generally for the aesthetic thought of the founders of Marxism, as distinguished from the writings of Plekhanov, Mehring, Lafargue, and other followers on art and literature (for a useful account see Z. G. Apresian, "An Appraisal of the Work Done in the 1930's on the Foundation of Marxist Esthetics," *Soviet Studies in Philosophy*, Spring 1967, pp. 39-50).

During the early 1930's, a number of the Marx and Engels texts, with commentaries, began to appear in Soviet magazines and in the Communist foreign-language press, e.g., *International Literature* (Moscow), read by leftwing authors and critics in the United States and England. The Russian collection of 1933 was the basis of selections brought out in French (1936), German (1937), Spanish (1946), and English (1947). Meanwhile an augmented, revised Russian edition was published in 1938, and, after World War II, Lifshitz edited the first fundamental collection in German (*Ueber Kunst und Literatur*, East Berlin, 1948) and an enlarged two-volume edition in Russian (Moscow, 1957). The most recent fundamental edition, the work of Manfred Kliem, appeared in East Berlin during 1967-68; it offers previously overlooked texts, but does not include some of the important ones found in the Lifshitz 1948 edition, nor is Kliem's plan of organization equal to that of Lifshitz.

As supplements to the above sources: the youthful poems, narratives, and aesthetic views of Marx and Engels are in the so-called *MEGA* (*Historisch-kritische Gesamtausgabe*, Frankfurt am Main, 1927-, I Abt., Bd. 1). Translations of some of these writings are included by Robert Payne in his Marx biography and in *The Unknown Karl Marx* (New York, 1971). (These texts of their youth are most fully interpreted by Auguste Cornu, *Karl Marx et Friedrich Engels, la vie et leurs oeuvres,* Paris, 1954-62.) Marx's readings in aesthetics prior to 1840 are known from letters only, since his earlier research notebooks are lost. They exist thereafter, however, and are surveyed to 1856 by Maximilien Rubel ("Les cahiers de lecture de Karl Marx," *International Review of Social History,* II, iii [1957], 392-418 and V, i [1960], 39-76). Finally one must mention *Freiligraths Briefwechsel mit Marx und Engels,* ed. M. Häckel (Berlin, 1968).

The following are the major interpretations of the aesthetic thought of Marx and Engels (together with essays which introduce the major compilations): Peter Demetz, *Marx, Engels, and the Poets* (Chicago, 1967; Ger. ed., Stuttgart, 1959; for a critique see L. Baxandall, *Partisan Review,* Winter 1968, pp. 152-156); Georgij M. Fridlender, *K. Marx i F. Engels i woprosi litjeraturi* (Moscow, 1962); Andrei N. Jezuitow, *Woprosi rjealizma w estjetike Marxa i Engelsa* (Moscow, 1963); Georg Lukács, *K. Marx und F. Engels als Literaturhistoriker* (Berlin, 1938) and *Beiträge zur Geschichte der Aesthetik* (Berlin, 1954), pp. 191-285; Pavel S. Trofimov, *Otsherki istorii marksistokoj estetiki* (Moscow, 1963), pp. 5-108) Hans Koch, *Marxismus und Aesthetik* (Berlin, 1962); Henri Lefèbvre, *Contribution a l'esthétique* (Paris, 1953); Adolfo Sánchez Vázques, *Art and Society: Essays in Marxist Aesthetics* (New York, 1974; Span. ed., Mexico City, 1965); Mikhail Lifshitz, *The Philosophy of Art of Karl Marx* (New York, 1938; Russ. ed., Moscow, 1933); Max Raphael, *Proudhon, Marx, Picasso* (Paris, 1933), pp. 123-185; W. C. Hoffenschefer, *Iz istorii marksistskoj kritiki* (Moscow, 1967), chaps. V and VI; Franz P. Schiller, *Engels kak literaturnij kritik* (Moscow, 1933); and Vera Machackova, *Der junge Engels und die Literatur* (Berlin, 1961).

II. *The Preliminary Problems*

Peter Demetz has sharply severed the aesthetic thought of Engels from that of Marx. He is not the only Western scholar to have done this. Marx is attributed with having broad European tastes—Engels, German and provincial preferences; Marx is said to have been cool or indifferent to realism while

Engels advocated it; and so on. What is true is that the home backgrounds and early years of the two men were distinctive and so, too, were their youthful enthusiasms. Engels was engrossed by the *Junges Deutschland* (Young Germany) movement, and he wanted to follow the example of its leading figures. Marx was acquainted at an early age with the classical literary heritage; eagerly absorbing it, he wrote poetry and studied philosophy and aesthetics at the University of Bonn where A. W. Schlegel was among his professors. Nevertheless, the early writings of both men indicate a converging development. With the start of their intimate collaboration (September 1844) the aesthetic standpoints grow together. One can speak confidently of a coalescence of their major aesthetic ideas; the unity of their approach to problems does not deny differences in their temperaments or in their special interests. Their individual emphases on certain topics and problems can easily be distinguished. Marx was more competent in abstract thought and was more systematic. Engels was more responsively sensitive and spontaneous. Where Marx was university-trained, the brilliant Engels was in large part self-educated. Marx's ideal (as Cornu characterizes it) was Prometheus and Engels', Siegfried of the *Nibelungenlied*. Yet, the growing-together of their approaches is evident—one cannot mistake it in the major critiques of Eugène Sue's *The Mysteries of Paris* (in *The Holy Family*, 1945) and Ferdinand Lassalle's drama *Franz von Sickingen* (see the 1859 correspondence with the author), where their views coincide even though they did not write their analyses in direct consultation.

Twice, Marx made plans to write systematically on aesthetics. In the winter of 1841-42 he worked with Bruno Bauer on a critique of Hegel's view of art and religion. Later he sought to comply with an 1857 bid from the *New American Cyclopedia* for an article on "Aesthetics" (evidently with that aim, he reviewed F. T. Vischer's works, E. Müller's history of ancient Greek aesthetics, and other writings). Neither undertaking was ever realized.

Accordingly, the question is left open as to how the texts of Marx and Engels on aesthetic matters should be organized. A chronological ordering would not in itself be especially enlightening. I will approach the matter by (a) discussing whether two phases, one pre-Marxian and the other Marxian, appear in their writings on art and literature and by (b) outlining the thematic patterns of structural coherences to be found among their many scattered ideas and comments.

Surely the former of these problems cannot be disposed of

without considering the general development of the Marxian philosophy and world view. In *Pour Marx* (Paris, 1966; English edition, 1970), Louis Althusser re-opened the controversy on the question of 'phases.' He regards *The German Ideology* as a *coupure épistémologique* (the term is Bachelard's) and states that this work abandoned the ambiguous idea of humanism in favor of a scientific, i.e., Marxist approach. The notion of such a 'cut-off point' seems, however, impossible to maintain. The efficacy of the Marxian world view does not consist in its presumed status as a pure science—for it is above all a philosophy of history, of which social science (empirically founded) is a constituent part, and both as philosophy of history and as social science obvious elements already appear in the Paris *1844 Manuscripts*. A solution contrary to Althusser's, and yet as extreme in character, was offered by Robert C. Tucker. The worst of Tucker's view of the general development of Marx's writings is that he misunderstands and distorts the ideas. Tucker argues in *Philosophy and Myth in Karl Marx* (London, 1961) that the theoretician and founder of the most widespread and successful political movement of workers was neither a sociologist, an economist, nor historian. Marx was —says Tucker—a prophet who overlooked the realities of life to project his visions onto the social universe; a moral philosopher, Marx dreamt of the 'aesthetic life' awaiting mankind. Tucker does make useful points in locating 'change within continuity' in Marx's and Engels' intellectual development. Yet, he excludes a significant treatment of key issues of Marxian philosophy and aesthetics; if his assumptions are correct, one hardly can take seriously their notions of the dependency of art on socioeconomic processes, the class context of the artist's origins and functions, or the dialectically founded discrepancy between the cultural and material levels of human development. But Tucker's assumptions are in error. And Marx, the student of history, has established more firmly than anyone that historical and sociological studies provide decisive insights into the permanent attributes and changes of art. That said, Tucker still does encourage us to see how much Marx, the philosopher of history, regarded the increase of artistic activity as a sure sign of human liberation.

To sum up: the intellectual development of Marx and Engels was neither purely scientific nor purely utopian—and, if we regard it with the analysis of either Tucker or Althusser, we shall distort it. Their concerns, deeply rooted in social observation, appear in late as well as early writings. These include: artistic freedom as opposed to alienation (dating from Marx's 1842 commentary on censorship); the proliferation of artistic activity in the epoch following class society, tied with art's emergence in the labor process (the *1844 Manuscripts*); and the discussion of 'tendency' writing (Engels on *Junges Deutschland*). One could chart these themes and dates in juxtaposition to their reemergence—or again, the character of aesthetic experience (linked to the rise of labor and art) in 1844 and in *Capital* (1867); realism, probed in 1859 and the 1880's; 'tendency,' in 1846-48 and the 1880's. No aesthetic issue, once raised, vanished; they all recurred, even if often in altered context. Because the continuities are demonstrable, I shall consider here the whole of their aesthetic thought starting at the end of 1842, when, despite the lasting traces of the thought of Hegel and Feuerbach, the founders of Marxism are well started in defining their distinctive world view. The process moved along rapidly in 1843, and at year's end, Marx already spoke of the "material force" of the emergent philosophy of history. If I insist on selecting the articles on creative liberty from the *Rheinische Zeitung* as the starting-point, it is because I find here (as M. Lifshitz and some other Marxologists do not) one of the abiding, fundamental themes of Marxist aesthetics. As the years passed, then, Marx and Engels made no basic changes of direction; instead, they established with deepened analyses the course they would pursue to reach the goal they had affirmed in 1842, when they were revolutionary democrats. The direction was always toward superseding the era of the coercive state, where people are regularly deprived of the right to "their own style." As Engels was to put it late in his life: the struggle led by the proletarian class against the capitalist system was sure to provide access for the whole of humanity to the "kingdom of freedom."

We are faced with another preliminary problem. How shall those brief, scattered texts on literature and art be systematized? As a precaution, and indeed, a central procedure, we should distinguish the writings which explicitly and coherently elaborate a topic from the fragments which contain a thesis about a topic but which leave it undeveloped in part and thus rather unclear, and, from the hasty or opaque comments which, as such, don't offer a reliable basis for a thesis. The first category may be termed the dominant themes of Marx and Engels; the second may be termed observations; the third, remarks. In the first category are to be found most of the issues providing the topic-headings in the selection of texts: i.e., the origin of aesthetic sensibility, the alienation which affects the artist and his work, the problem of realism, 'tendency' writing, the class equivalents of art. (I may point out that each of these dominant themes—with the exception of the first—is concerned with art's functional aspects, and these correspond to specific attributes of artistic structures.) Among the semi-finished themes of the second category, we find: the distinguishing traits of aesthetic objects and aesthetic experience; the recurrent attributes and enduring values of art; the comic and the tragic; form and style. The third category, comprised of brief comments, includes topics such as the distinction between science and art, the role of philosophy in artistic creation, and the hierarchy of artistic values.

The sustained treatments by Marx and Engels of the Sue novel and the *Sickingen* play by Lassalle are, not surprisingly, a prime textual source for the dominant themes. The general methodological assumptions and procedures are best interpreted and oriented to these dominant themes. On the other hand, a grave injustice would be done to the breadth and complexity of Marxian aesthetic thought if we excluded the second and third categories of materials from the patterning of the *disiecta membra*. Therefore, where appropriate, the major topics can be amplified by this material.

III. *General Methodological Assumptions and Dominant Themes*

Many propositions of Marxian aesthetic thought are far from generally agreed upon today. The debates among those who write on the topics can be sharp, but there is some agreement on a few propositions, and something like consensus on one key formulation which we may state as follows: Aesthetic phenomena are studied in a context of socio-historical processes, and in this way are regarded as part of a broad, "civilizational" activity by which the species *homo sapiens* advances slowly to realize an innate potential. Art objects are not isolated phenomena, but are mutually dependent with other cultural activity of predominantly social, political, moral, religious, or scientific character. But how shall we describe the dynamics of the interdependence with these other fields of human endeavor? This mutuality is of dual character: in current parlance it is a synchronic dynamism, transacted in a given moment of the constituted structure of society, and it is also a diachronic dynamism, with the givens of the past being reconsidered by and affecting the present, and the future. Why do the fluctuations occur in what is highly appreciated or acknowledged in the aesthetic field? Basically, Marxism says this is due to changes in the ideology, i.e., systems of thought which are delimited by human interests, and accordingly in attitudes toward the givens. Ideologies, which are always highly complex, are conditioned in the last instance by the pervasive contradictions and general evolution of the class-divided societies of history. There is, however, besides ideology, another chief factor influencing the change of attitudes toward aesthetic phenomena; this is the contradiction which repeatedly asserts itself between settled ideology and the attitudes which individuals freshly discover in assessing the human social and natural situation—and which have a powerful emotional and volitional potential. We may speak of these latter sources of contradiction as 'psychosocial,' and perhaps as 'mythological,' in character.

This, very briefly, is the context and the dynamic of art phenomena, as Marxian thought specifically conceives them. In addition, the dynamism occurs in two separate fields of interdependence. These are the idiogenetic setting of influence, where new aesthetic activity is affected by *previous aesthetic* models; and, the allogenetic setting, where *non-aesthetic* givens have influence on new artistic activity. This may appear obvious; but the distinction is worth making clear at once.

These elements of mutuality in a context and of dynamics of change cohere into a methodological position when one seeks to approach the various problems posed by aesthetic objects and aesthetic activity. The best name for the approach is: *historicism*. The framework of Marxian aesthetic thought is, then, historicist. We may ask how the dominant themes of Marx's and Engels' aesthetic thought are clarified as we orient them by historicism. One dominant theme, already noted, concerns the birth, or genesis, of art; and four other dominant themes relate to the functions of art. None of these can be adequately understood apart from historical data which affect the traits and changes of art.

For instance—we consider *the genesis of art* (of artistic sensibility) in a context which includes the historical activity of *homo sapiens* as a whole. What are we able to find? The peculiar phenomena of this field emerge in the closest connection with the survival activity of our species at a primitive level; the phenomena then pursue a checkered course through the pressures and interests of our historical, class-striated societies; the specifically-focused energy of the activity of art is continually sustained by the undying and evolving human wish for freedom from coercion, injustice, hunger, and chaos. This analysis of the developmental context leads by a seamless transition, we see, to the problem (and dominant theme) of the *class context* and *class equivalents* of the phenomena, as these functionally emerge. In the broadest, most profound and ongoing aspect, the class mutuality of art with its social contexts has to be described as its *alienation*, together with that of its makers and users. By the same token, the potent energies which renew art may, in their most profound aspect, be considered to strive for its eventual *disalienation*, but again only in a total human and historical context. Disalienation would find *homo faber*, working humanity, gain the cooperative ability to go beyond exhausting toil in oppressed conditions to adopt social relations which more resemble play. Active then as *homo aestheticus* (among other basic traits), this future humanity might freely and creatively achieve the realization of the totality of potential faculties.

Does the Marxian historical approach deny that aesthetic ideas and artistic expression possess a relative autonomy, as they develop in various distinguishable traditions? Not at all! On the other hand—*realism* is common in art and literature; so is the evidence of the artist's sociopolitical *'tendency,'* asserted or implicit; and these phenomena manifest the historical process and its ideological patterns, which anyway are latent in art.

A full treatment by Marxian historicism of artistic realism and 'tendency' in art will bring in three related ideas or themes, which lend this part of the approach much of its breadth and dynamism. I mean the emphasis given by Marx and Engels to human labor, which conditions and makes culture possible; the insistence that social revolutions have their place, as unavoidable and therefore desirable links in the progress of the species; and the contention that the communist commitment is both an ideal that humanity adopts, and a real, historically applicable means of advancing that change. The reader should have seen earlier how fundamental labor, for Marx and Engels, is both the primordial activity from which aesthetic sensibility may develop, and a conditioning matrix which never ceases to impinge to some extent on artistic creation. The ideas and feelings which contribute to social revolution, judged an integral part of history and at times central to human activity, are of course seen as appropriate for artistic representation. It is nothing new for poetry to acquire stature as a kind of 'legislator' or tribune on behalf of suffering humanity, and it is widely accepted that when the social awareness of material conditions spreads, change becomes possible; Marx and Engels simply describe this function in terms of their philosophy of history and the communist ideal. Their historicism enables us to see, finally, how this function is fulfilled or fails, in the way people propose ideas and artistic methods which they either have grown capable of enacting or they envision as leading to early success (the 'utopian' transcendence of the problem). Unfortunately, in many cases, the utopian glance forward mystifies the social reality of the present (art included); a *camera oscura* effect looks upside-down at the mutually dependent elements, with the result that symptomatic aspects (ideological, artistic, etc.) may be asserted as the basis on which all else rests, or moves. In short: mystification (whether of the conformist or the utopian variety) may dull the awareness which could arouse or perhaps even point the way for historical change.

Another aspect of Marxian historicism must be mentioned in understanding the dominant aesthetic themes; I mean the explicit notion that the idea of progress of the species must be qualified by recognition that there has been an unequal development of the cultural as compared with the economic and technical fields. We would be completely perplexed in describing and estimating historically early art if we assumed its attainment must correspond to the material level in its time. On the other hand, modern art is created in a genetic framework of higher achievement and complexity (religious, philosophical, scientific, technical, etc.), which offers no guarantee that the present aesthetic achievement can match that of olden times. The oddity of this unequal development seems, in some part, to stem from the collective endeavors and myths of antiquity, and the extreme individualism of artistic work in capitalist times. This last factor also encourages the enlarged place for chance and accident in modern art. The phenomenon also helps explain why old artistic 'forms' are often borrowed for new uses (cf. Marx's letter of July 22, 1861 to Lassalle, where he discusses the misunderstanding of Greek drama by the seventeenth-century French dramatists who made ample use of its forms). The notion furthermore adds perspective to modern debates on art vs. science and art vs. industrialism. Writing on the theme of the *Ende der Kunstperiode* ('the end of the era of art') in the *People's Paper* of April 19, 1856, Marx showed himself the apt pupil of Hegel's views in this matter—but also the originator of a wholly new diagnosis of the decline. Certainly, the principle of unequal development between the 'spiritual' and material fields saves Marxian historicism from a blind assertion of progress; especially in aesthetic matters.

In these ways, art emerges and functions as a *specific mode of the social consciousness.* As for the work of art by the *individual artist,* it is distinguished from the general social consciousness in further ways: (a) desires and beliefs which often are mutually contradictory, not fully rational, are important; (b) a pervasive effect is established by the individual artist's vision, even granting its development in social context; and (c) nature, both within and outside, as experienced by the artist, is freshly opposed to the general social consciousness. Although mediated by culture, the juxtaposition represents an innocent seeing of the nature which is 'beyond.' The artist seeks to acculturate nature anew, and on the other hand, to naturalize culture. He hardly can avoid doing this while encountering reality in his time.

So far, I have treated the dominant aesthetic themes of Marx and Engels in order to illuminate the methodological approach which is continually brought to bear on them. It is now possible to turn the attention around, to closely scrutinize the dominant aesthetic themes in light of the governing methodology.

Again I remind my reader that we are treating *disiecta membra.* The ideas of Marx and Engels about literature and the other arts are scattered in passages which we must organize, *reconstruct* as to their coherence. I shall draw on the texts which seem most relevant to major problems and solutions of European aesthetic thought up to the present. On the other side, the aesthetic thought of Marx and Engels is integrally joined with their world view and philosophy of history. This contextual integration has been interpreted in two ways, which, mutually incompatible, must both be rejected. The first says that the Marxian approach to art and literature is 'extrinsic'—*only* general-philosophical or *only* sociopolitical. The other says that *all* of communist thought is aesthetic—see Tucker—a Schillerian anthropology more or less, with the ideal *des spielenden Menschen.* This assertion is especially objectionable because Tucker sees the 'aesthetic' pervasion as metaphysical and without a functional relation to empirical data.

The Chief Aesthetic Problems Considered by Marx and Engels

a. *The Origin of Aesthetic Sensibility*

Marx's treatment of the origin of aesthetic sensibility could not be sufficiently developed or tested by empirical data, which in his time were still scarce. Therefore, he developed a philosophical argument using available knowledge, as did other authors. Marx implicitly aimed his analysis against the theistic and naturalistic positions. He rejected the *je ne sais quoi* arguments of seventeenth-century thinkers as much as he disputed an instinct that was peculiarly aesthetic and divinely-endowed or naturally-endowed.

Marx explained aesthetic sensibility as very gradually taking shape among the specific formations of concrete historical processes—foremostly as part of the development of human labor. Artistic creation and aesthetic response are specifically human capabilities for Marx. They should not be confused with phenomena in the animal world that resemble them. *Homo faber*—laboring humanity—first gains and then refines aesthetic sensibility while improving work skills and mastering the material world through idea and activity. What is earliest achieved is the active artistic competence. The physical world is reworked to the harmonious standard, use, or measure (*Mass*) of humanity. Meanwhile, because the aesthetic skills are developed, the (humanized) play capacity finds new outlets: *Spiel seiner eignen körperlichen und geistigen Kräfte.* To this extent the *homo faber* is on the way to becoming *homo ludens.*

If then we want to talk about the aesthetic sensibility in its more contemplative aspect—i.e., the stricter or at least the more usual sense—we shall have to consider it a later development which derives from the art-formative phase. Marx once used the term "mineralogical sense" to describe an attitude which was aesthetically receptive to precious natural objects because it involved a more or less apractical detachment from the other possible functions. This mode of receptivity is describable as an interiorization of the sensibility which is needed by those who make artistic artefacts. As such it is a counterpart of the preceding process of human exteriorization which is artistic production. As the dialectic of exteriorization/interiorization continues, the artistic patterns that evolve and the proto-aesthetic responses which these evoke build increasingly conspicuous relationships. Thus, a specifically aesthetic attitude is formed. The above account is greatly supported by Marx's general theory of the process by which primitive humanity turns material reality to its needs through a process of appropriation (*Aneignung*) which is both objective and subjective. Among a number of functional attitudes, a specifically human aesthetic sensibility (which is first nothing but actively artistic) is generated by the total social praxis as the species affirms and realizes its "human essence."

Briefly, this is the theoretical framework of the genesis of aesthetic sensibility which may be reconstructed from the texts of Marx. If we now turn to some of the relevant texts we shall both grasp the theme more firmly and see the interpretive difficulties. In the *1844 Manuscripts* and *A Contribution to the Critique of Political Economy* Marx discusses precious gold and silver objects; he states that their hues constitute "aesthetic properties" which stimulate "the most popular form of aesthetic sense." We note that Marx calls color attributes popular but not the most rudimentary mode of aesthetic stimuli historically. None the less, does this mean that Marx locates a *natural* foundation for aesthetic response in these sensuously experienced, physical color traits? In other texts Marx discusses structural attributes, i.e., those historically evolved in the labor process (the humanized *Mass*, 'measure,' of the object), as the basis of the aesthetic response. Does this conflict with, or qualify, the observation on the hues of metals? Should we perhaps speak of *two* Marxian parallel categories—one consisting of color constituted aesthetic properties that appeal to a naturally-endowed capacity enjoyed by a labor-developed humanity? I believe this suggestion is ill-founded; if we study the *1844 Manuscripts* and *Capital* we can have no grounds to accept a naturally-endowed aesthetic response which *homo faber* preserves intact through its development. We shall perhaps do better if we try to reconstruct Marx's idea of the stages of emergence of the aesthetic sensibility. I propose the following as a fair outline:

(a) At first, art developed; it was a kind of bonus as primitive workers formed objects for use and in general exercised and expressed their power to master the material world.

(b) After much time, the structure of the object (its inherent *Mass*, measure, proportion) could come to chiefly occupy the artisan's attention. At this stage, obsessive functionalism started to fade, and apractical aesthetic contemplation could begin to emerge.

(c) Aesthetic responsiveness to 'given' physical attributes such as color, timbre, etc., could develop at a later time when the aesthetic sensibility had become pronounced, relatively autonomous, and internally various. It would occur as a subsequent phase of this rudimentary process which is generated by human labor and centered on human labor, from which art and its subjective counterparts are generated. Marx's world view suggests to us that the overall process would require millions of years—spanning from the early paleolithic to the late neolithic era.

If we turn now to observations by Marx on the traits by which we distinguish art objects and aesthetic experience, some support and also amplification can be found for this reconstruction of the stages through which the aesthetic sensibility was generated. In the *1844 Manuscripts*, the objective mode of the beautiful is said to be its *'Mass,'* measure. Similarly, the *Grundrisse der Kritik der politischen Oekonomie* speaks of compact structure—*'geschlossene Gestalt, Form und gegebene Begrenzung'*—as the main characteristic of Greek art. Certainly, the German word *'Mass'* which Marx uses is correlated to his general world view, and has to be interpreted in various contexts. Here, it appears to mean: (a) reproduction of the *structures of physical reality* (their shapes mainly; primitive people found that in mastering these shapes, they also gained the best way to make tools, pots, shelter, etc.); and, (b) various specific attributes of symmetry, regularity, proportion, and harmony, which provide an attractive and coherent whole such as differs from—or more exactly, *rivals*—the shapes of material reality. But whatever else *'Mass'* meant for Marx, in aesthetic context this term definitely indicates an *inner compact structure* of the work of art. This is so even where there is attention directed to reproduction of the outward structure of real objects. Marx's word 'reproduction' where he speaks of the correlated emergence of the human capacities and the essential attributes of art should accordingly be kept very distinct from 'realism.' How could he possibly have conceived of this 'reproduction' as mimesis at the beginnings of aesthetic phenomena? No writer of the mid-nineteenth century knew the earliest cave art. Marx was preoccupied by the mythology in ancient Greek art, and he and Engels both described how primitive religions misshaped and suffused art. In neither era could a 'measured' reproduction of the real world have been called realism. To Marx and Engels, realism was the aim of a particular and much later literary school or artistic emphasis—and it definitely was far from the basis of art. Rather, the Marxian idea of realism referred mainly to a typifying social representation. It did not connote fundamental formal structure, nor did it go back to the origin of art.

Their other concerns later in life kept Marx and Engels from further exploring the primordial formal structure in relation to the material world, we see through their 1859 letters on Lassalle's *Sickingen* play they did not lose interest in the formal problems. As for later investigations by Marxists, Lukács is most ample—treating mimesis as the fundamental principle (*Die Eigenart des Aesthetischen*, 1963); Lukács is too anxious, however, to provide the concept of *'Mass,'* measure, with an inclusive mimetic meaning. All true art is for him mimetic, and Lukács claims Marx as his witness. If we accept this conception then mimesis becomes a very vague and malleable phenomenon indeed. We see, moreover, how Lukács himself describes the development of mimetic art as occurring only because there was also a primitive emergence of relatively autonomous structures (which he calls the *Für-sich-Sein* of art). Although Lukács insists on the primacy of mimesis, he acknowledges the need for a certain internal organization of the magico-symbolic 'artistic content'—which is of a proportionate character within a structure having relative autonomy.

Let us look more closely at the relatively autonomous structure of art. I think Marx's observations in the matter bear out my interpretation rather than Lukács. A dealer (says Marx in the *1844 Manuscripts*) sees the market for precious stones but not their beauty. Amplifying, Marx observes (*Contribution*) that the aesthetic pleasure afforded by a diamond on a woman's bosom is lacking when the same stone is regarded as a commodity. In the former instance the "aesthetic use-value" is apparent, in other circumstances the stone's exchange-value rather than its specificity may prevail. Its aesthetic use-value is also, of course, distinct from the "mechanical" use-value of a diamond in "the hand of a glasscutter." We see, in its context, that the aesthetic use-value is a specific quality of the object, and directly gratifies a concrete human need. The apractical character of aesthetic experience is further brought out by several observations in *Capital* which primarily excoriate the odious experience of work in capitalist society. In a passage on ungratifying factory labor, for instance, Marx says the worker is deprived of "enjoying the work as a play of his own mental and physical powers." He says of medieval handicraft in the *Grundrisse:* "this work is still half artistic, it has still the aim in itself (*Selbstzweck*)." Surely, we are barred by these foregoing passages from lending a basically utilitarian teleology to Marx's concept of aesthetic experience. On the other hand, they don't head off the interpretation that mimesis is the primary element of aesthetic experience. And yet, I think it is not insignificant that Marx nowhere encourages this interpretation. Moreover, he makes much of the idea that human activity, in its specifically human aspect, stands apart from nature. The *1844 Manuscripts* declare that humanity "confronts" (gains a distance on) the materials and the aims which it is productive. Unlike other species, our species acts according to the laws of beauty, adopting a due concern for the inherent measure of the object; in this way the human species "only truly produces in freedom" from immanent nature and abject need. I suggest that only on the basis of this freedom, too, can one conceive the making of an apractical, relatively autonomous world of art.

However, it should be noted here that Marx regards aesthetic experience as synthetic in character: a mingling of the intellectual, emotional, and sensual. This permits the presence of intensive mimetic material as 'artistic content' without disturbing the apractical structure of the work of art. On the other hand, while a synthesis of such aspects, its reception is non-discursive, i.e., atheoretical. For instance, in the 1859 preface to the *Contribution*, Marx distinguishes the intellectual and religious appropriations of reality from the artistic one. An 1858 letter scoffing at Arnold Ruge's rejection of Shakespeare finds worthless his notion that the presence of a "philosophical system" could give the edge to a work of art. Certainly the cognition which distinctively occurs in art is unlike other modes of cognition.

Does this distinctiveness of art objects also preclude ethical concerns as they are evidenced outside art? One might indeed tend to say so, from the way the pietistic moralism of Eugène Sue was ridiculed as inappropriate to the telling of his story. On the other hand, although Marx and Engels might jibe at morally callow authors who made their ethical judgments stridently central to their work, none the less they acknowledged an implicit moral superiority in certain human activities as compared with others, and they were committed to a human ideal which art's own central character contributed to realizing, on the one hand by its mere manifestation, and on the other hand as the medium for representations of the ethical ideals of humanity being recognized or realized. Here was an appropriate integration of aesthetic phenomena with moral perspective.

In sum, there has evolved since the genesis of aesthetic sensibility a situation where an object and a subject constitute together an aesthetic field. For the time of the transaction, each is somehow a self-sufficient, harmonious structure involved by the field, because at the time relatively autonomous from other functions and the greater world. The subject and object together make a 'rival' world with its own distinctive traits—the 'autotelicism' does not, however, preclude cognitive and ideological aspects, and, on the whole, both the specific integration of the art object, and the unique resultant experience which enriches the psyche, retain links with the ordinary world and other human experience that are never severed.

In this treatment of the origin of art, I have reinforced the interpretation by also drawing on the observations of Marx and Engels as to the distinguishing traits of works of art and of aesthetic experience. It is also appropriate to consider in this place their observations concerning form and style. Form they considered as the whole of the artistic means—the necessary harmonious organization of the parts which constitutes a whole artistic structure. They wrote little on problems of form, and this is explained only in part by Engels' letter of 1893 to Mehring, where he says he and Marx were bound to lay emphasis first on content; more than this (and as the *Sickingen* letters confirm), they gave primacy to content; theirs is a *Gehaltästhetik*. Need I stress again that this statement in no way invalidates their underlying assumption that the work of art is an autotelic structure, experienced with a relative autonomy?

Style, in the treatment of both Marx and Engels, is the imprint of the individual artistic personality on the work of art. Neither said enough theoretically about the characteristics of style for us to connect what they said on the style of this or that artist to their thought on other aesthetic matters.

b. *Alienation and Disalienation of Art*

Productive labor provided not only the originating conditions of aesthetic activity and art. The latter have been decisively affected through history by the processes of development among employers and working people as a whole, together with the ensuing patterns of consumption by the various classes of society of the products of labor. Marx gave his attention chiefly to the capitalist era of culture and production, as he did in so many matters. But now and then he did comment on the artist's situation in other eras, and it seems proper to conclude that in the aesthetic field, too, he regarded alienation as integrated into the development of civilization up to the present. Looked at from the standpoint of progress of the human species, the progress has been paid for in distorting side-effects. Progress beyond the animal status was at the cost of engendering oppression, exploitation, and character disorder. Through this rigorous and inexorable civilizational dynamic, aesthetic activity and art objects were both developed and forced into patterns partially thwarting their potential realization. This is what the term alienation signifies. The alienation of art from its intrinsic potential complemented and gave aid to related fields for alienation: religious, political, etc.

Yet, if alienation has been inseparable from aesthetic phenomena in all historical eras, it undoubtedly became more intensive, in Marx's judgment, as the market conditions of capitalism developed. The capitalist market transformed art into a commodity, which it had never before been. An unknown purchaser would now be the source of the maker's livelihood. The pricing of the artefact would become a foremost factor. Where there had been a community of interests, values, tastes, and knowledge, now the need to depersonalize, and incentives to calculate as to the market and its buyers, became important. Moreover, what grouping was most isolated from the maker of art objects? Clearly, it was the industrial working class, those who were the producers of the other commodities for the market. Laboring men and women had originated and long pursued aesthetic activity and art in a past grown irretrievable; their most direct descendents now lacked the time-off and surplus income to relate to art, which had, due to specialization and alienation, now to be produced by a remote stratum of experts.

What were the fundamental traits of the alienation processes during the capitalist era in particular, as described by Marx and Engels? These aspects may be specified as applying *inter alia* to the field of the arts, but never separable from the effects of alienation in other domains. The consequences in one field would moreover be felt through all of society, by persons of every degree and vocation.

1. *Homo faber*, the working person, is separated from the product of work. For the most part, the product may not be kept, used, enjoyed, or distributed by the producer. *Disposal of the product is at the discretion of owners of capital* who have organized its production or marketing. Profit is the aim.

2. Competition for profits also determines the internal character of the production process. There is usually *a tempo, repetition, uniformity, etc., in the order of work which enslave the maker of the object.* Rote labor defeats creative initiative.

3. *Human individual and species-potential itself must be misshapen* when thus oppressed and exploited to achieve the needs of profit for the owners of capital. Alienation takes those

who are at work further and further away, not only from their natural capacities and propensities, but even from the recognition of these.

This description to some extent touches on the alienation of working people in every kind of productive activity; and it embraces to some degree every era of class-divided socio-economic relations. If the reader thinks for example of the modern film industry, the best-selling novel industry, or the theatre business, the alienational aspect is apparent. Yet, the artist-expert has been given many advantages in every era; once the sale-value of his work is acknowledged, he is manifoldly compensated for the discomforts of having to submit to alienation. It is otherwise for the industrial worker who is considered interchangeable, part of a reserve factory force. And indeed, artists may be tempted to respond: "Alienation can't get a hold on me, as I give my art the highest priority, and whether it makes a lot of money for me doesn't matter. I choose my own themes and methods, I put the whole of my being into my artistic work, and I will let it go into the world only on my own terms." However, the more recognized and successful the artist, the less likely, on the whole, has it been that he could claim free and full control over the disposal of his product, the conditions and intentions of his work, and its correspondence to his natural or spontaneous potential. Both factory worker and artist are of course 'free' to withhold their participation; one can sleep under a bridge, one can apply for welfare payments. If one does not imagine that aloofness to the marketplace and deprivation of a living income is true freedom, then the market in another of its ramifications will set the pre-conditions for even the most skilled, energetic, resourceful, and rebellious activity. Even the stubbornest of artists must either forego most of the socio-economic resources available to more amenable artists of the day, or else submit to recalculating all aspects of the original impulses to artistic activity, on a basis of their contribution to success in terms of the market and its buyers—the patrons and public of today.

The isolation of the artist, especially from the more responsive and supportive community of an earlier era, coupled with exacerbated conditions of oppression and conflict in society, has had mixed results. As Marx observed, the pre-conditions for some kinds of artistic activity virtually disappeared: no longer could a Milton spin out poetry as a spider might a web. Neither the workers nor the middle class were an apt audience for retaining the inheritance of art or for welcoming innovations. On the other hand, recognizing the flagrant dangers for aesthetic activity, the artist might take refuge in a bohemian community where, with other artists, he could pursue some cherished if still partly blighted projects. Dialectically, bohemia would, in its turn, become the attractive community of nonconforming ways of life-style for growing numbers of non-artists. Or again, while the rote or machine reproduction of *objets d'art* for the home undoubtedly lowered the standards of many involved in this work, yet the *objets* as assuredly raised or broadened the aesthetic experience of many middle and lower-middle class families. Some varieties of expression were thus democratized while they were homogenized and merchandised. Similarly, the *Communist Manifesto* noted a gain for literature from the capitalist world market: national boundaries took a beating, and world literature became a fact. On the whole, it may be said that the deteriorization of the earlier communities for which art was conceived and by which it was received had a releasing effect on individual expression. The solitary artist could see more possibilities than those which group conformity sanctioned; unprecedented works could be attempted without immediate fear of reactions, beyond the loss of that impersonal, often supremely disinterested market. Yet even the most audacious and achieved art of the capitalist era was marked by its setting. The fullest aesthetic potential seemed unrealized. The anguish of the artists was frequently a part of its complexion. And the best of this art was seldom accessible to more than a small elite; while others living in the era, including the average industrialist, merchant, or banker, got along on commercialized trash and spectacles designed above all to reap profits.

No wonder, then, that Marx and Engels preferred ancient art. They regarded the Greek achievements as unsurpassed. The Renaissance and Middle Ages, too, in their opinion had given more propitious conditions to art than did the nineteenth century. At that time, at least the alienation might have been mitigated by the artist's wholehearted participation in the class opinions of his patron; and the patrons were moreover often generous with commissions and non-interfering in their execution. By the mid-nineteenth century, many artists found the new patrons of the arts unbearable, and in fury or hope, they even were siding with the aspirations of the lower classes.

This is something of the historical dynamic which emerged as the alienation induced by civilizational development began to intensify. But Marxian philosophy did not leave the dynamic at that; it drew forth the *disalienational* processes from the intensified alienation of the present, and cautiously speculated where they might lead. The movement towards full disalienation and towards communism was identified. And this era, when productive individuals would enjoy the processes and the results of their work as the realization of their innate powers, was seen to coincide with the social superseding of the whole of history until then, considered as an epoch of socio-economic scarcity; in other words, the era of cooperation in realizing human needs and goals would depend on an unprecedented and democratized mastery of the problems set by nature and society. This was the expectation, and of course not only for aesthetic projections and fulfillment but in every field of human action. But what particularly of the aesthetic field? Marx, in fact, suggested that its scope would broaden out under more favorable socio-economic conditions, and, indeed, some of the specific aesthetic values would suffuse other fields as was the case in primitive society. A humanity grown productive and knowledgeable beyond any previous standards would be able to claim its birthright—also as *homo ludens*. Not attempting any detailed prediction, Marx mentioned three elements regarding this expectation:

1. The creative abilities of individuals would be fully developed; everyone capable of becoming a Raphael might do so.

2. The character of work would become increasingly aesthetic; its future would be *Selbstbetätigung*, a free play of the physical and psychic faculties.

3. Every person would grow capable of artistic achievement in every domain of the arts; there would no longer be professional painters but only painting as one pursuit in which everyone might participate.

Approaching such speculations today, in a context of the Marxian analysis of alienation and disalienation, what shall we think of them? The last of the three, which is earliest mentioned in *The German Ideology* and probably comes out of Fourier's *papillon* theory, recurs as late as Engels' *Anti-Dühring* despite some critical remarks on the Fourierist utopia. Can we single out any one, or two, of the three points for prime emphasis? I think not. The danger of a one-sided interpretation is visible in *Marx, penseur de la technique* (Paris, 1962), where the author, Kostas Axelos, not only gives foremost emphasis to the aesthetic suffusion of labor (*Arbeit als freies Spiel*), but he suggests that Marx anticipated a disappearance of the art object. If this were so, the Marxian disalienation would paradoxically provide a retrograde utopia, an atavistic lapse into the time when aesthetic structure had still to be consciously developed. In other respects Axelos' vision is a dimming of the Marxian original into a mere reverie on the idea of technological benefits. In my view, Marx unquestionably anticipated each of the three elements of aesthetic disalienation, and a communist revaluation of all values and vitalization of all reified processes would not promise anything less. We may still ask in how far, from our present vantage point, the expectations were firmly projected.

We cannot say with precision to what degree Marx and Engels should be seen as utopians in their speculation on aesthetic disalienation. The future can alone tell. I will venture, however, that they were rash in thinking that artistic specialization could disappear, and artistic capacities would be distributed evenly through the population (the third point). But if this was mostly wishful thinking, we can do no less than acknowledge the great prescience of Marx and Engels on point two when we consider today's tendencies to industrial art, happenings, the wedding of art directly to technology, the increased infusion of leisure with creativity. This aspect of Marxian philosophy now first truly coming into its own has been emphasized by Herbert Marcuse, starting with his *Essay on Liberation*; if Marcuse was at first drawn to the Axelos kind of interpretation, he has lately argued that the art object, as locus of form, will not disappear.

Most important in considering the disalienation theme, perhaps, is to remember that Marx and Engels were not given to prophecy as their method of inquiry. To examine their writings is to find few thoughts on the character of the future communist society. This absence of precise specification is not due, as Tucker alleges, to the lack of real grounds for their analysis and a substitution of vague messianism. The reason for reticence is their dislike of pontification. The advent of communism seemed economically and socially assured on the basis of the course of historical development in their analysis of it. This would certainly mean the end of alienation, as the conditions for it disappeared. But still, the advent of communist economic and social relations would provide but the basis, the threshold for the new epoch—the "pre-condition of freedom." In place of prognistications Marx and Engels concentrated their energies on the analysis of existing capitalism and the dynamic it evinced for changing. The prime dynamic factor seemed to be the needs and latent capacities of the oppressed in capitalism; once the subordination of the "stupid masses" to the "burdened geniuses" who controlled their destinies was overthrown, the times would be ripe for the emergence of *homo aestheticus.*

Yet, the notion of *homo aestheticus* in even the most tentative formulations will be rejected by some critics as an unwarranted extrapolation from what we know about the capacities of our species. There is nothing in the hope for an expanded artistic activity and freely playful spontaneity in work and leisure, these critics say. For instance, Tucker ascribes exaggeration to Marx's anticipation of an enriched human being who will appropriate the world with a fullness of the senses and "in need of a totality of human life-activities." Tucker does note the suggestion of hyperbole in the words Marx uses, but can he be right about the main issue? I think he misses the substantial historical point: that people can someday realize the potential which the existing social conditions suppress and distort. Indeed, is this a refutable thesis? The very mundane proof of it which is seen everywhere today has the effect of encouraging the risks which lead to further confirmation.

Another error which Tucker exhibits with aplomb: the disalienated personality is not to be reduced to an aesthetic personality. This violates the rounded, integrated Marxian vision. To be sure, Marx emphasizes aesthetic fulfillment, but in a greater totality, which is inherent to the historical dialectics of its conception. Thus, Tucker's chapters 14 and 15 depict the aesthetic liberation as coming out of the alienated self which has been rootless in alienated circumstances. But in Marx the process is considered as proceeding from the social action of persons in disalienating their circumstances. The communist individual is actualized—that is, goes from an *Unwesen* to a *menschlichen Wesen*—by transformational activity within a community and by a nature, which have been prepared by advances of humanity as a whole. In other words: the disalienated condition is as dependent on ethical, intellectual, and practical aspects as on aesthetic fulfillment.

Looking in another direction, the notions of disalienation and aesthetic realization have urgent bearing for the discussion of the Communist Person. Certainly, the endeavor to build Communist circumstances and personality has a decisive basis in ethical dedication, positive socio-economic theory, and practical experience—but it would be erroneous to omit appropriate attention to aesthetic activity and art in a socialist-based situation. The status of the arts must not be more goal-oriented and communicative than it is authentically artistic. On one page of the *1844 Manuscripts*, discussing the terrible power of commercial values to twist all other values, Marx says, "If you want to enjoy art, you must be an artistically cultured person." It must seem an obvious remark. But it does assume a developed capability of the Communist whole personality, which some influential persons in those circumstances are not prepared to encourage, because they demand a solely communicative art of the socialist perspective. Surely Marx's words serve as a rebuke to those who justify a massive propaganda inculcation of the population through "the arts," while penalizing or silencing the artists who will not adapt themselves to this single purpose.

c. *Class Values Embodied in Art*

Alienation and disalienation are quite evidently themes that are inseparably bound together in the thought of Marx and Engels. As for the remaining dominant themes of their aesthetic thought, these can be said to expand on the topics of alienation and disalienation, to the extent that a given work of art contains or embodies an ideological dimension. Ideology will here be considered as the statement or symptomatic expression of a pattern of social-class attitudes, interests, or habits of thought. When ideology is exhibited indirectly, as symptomatic expression, the artist may or may not be aware of having adopted a position. Such patterns may be elucidated by the experienced, careful, and knowledgeable critic, also in some cases where the work of art offers no portrayal of class interests in conflict and it adopts no tendentious position. Whatever the class or social values held and manifested by the artist, their motivation or cause will lie in the alienation which afflicts art and social life.

From the standpoint of alienation, some class values must be called morbid. These are the conscious or unconscious values which speak for the interests of the status quo in the patterns of a dominating class which has grown reactionary. Other works of art will oppose the alienated conditions, either latently or manifestly, with values approximating those of a particular class. Their phrases or their basic values may correspond to the attitudes of social classes that have not yet won their 'place in the sun,' historically—or whose class hegemony has earlier come and gone. The more rebellious the artist then the more likely to be deliberated are his aesthetic choices having class or social implication—and he may prove subject to many inner conflicts as compared with artists who rely on the more or less unexamined, ruling values in composing their works. Of course, the dissenting or revolutionary artist is also in danger of arrest, persecution, or ostracism from sources of livelihood and outlets which provide recognition and influence. An alternative course of dissent from ruling-class values is more implicit: the artist may choose to put up an 'ivory tower' as a rejection of market enticements or demands, and also of involvement with an overtly ideological stance of dissent. The problem is that the context of alienated social conditions creeps into the work anyway, as numerous examples of 'ivory tower' art testify. Whether a 'rebel' or a 'formalist,' then, the artist opposed to ruling-class values bears some cost for living when he does. It is a cost of different complexion from that chargeable to artists who acquiesce in ruling-class values. We could call the 'rebels' the counter-alienated. They are not reinforcers of the status quo values, or not of all of them. But in striving for ideological clarity and an ethical rigor, they risk neglect of some of the specific resources of art. The 'ivory tower' artist runs another type of risk, if also related to the specific matter of which art is composed: by turning away from the study of social relations, this artist often impoverishes his result; and the thinness of its content may even be set off with lumps of undigested, random ideology.

Considering ways in which specific resources of aesthetic objects can be misshapen, it is important to note that Marx and Engels approached class values present in works by individual authors in terms equally applicable, for instance, to texts by scholars or journalists. At the level of 'content' explication the medium's distinctive traits were set aside. Yet these traits and their vulnerability were mentioned at a more general plane, when they did analyze particular works of art in light of the entirety of the alienation diagnostic: for instance, more than once they suggested that an aggressively ideological clarity in anti-establishment poetry disturbed the structural autotelicism. Or take the much-quoted passage from Marx on the enduring values of ancient Greek art (in the *Contribution*), which clearly says that the truths of that day must be reproduced in our own art at a higher plane. By truth (*seine Wahrheit zu reproduzieren*) in art we may be certain that Marx did not mean an ideologically guiding or, again, a 'proletarian' art. With its commitment to arduous political goals and even to tactically detailed tasks, such art would better be seen as a means of preparing for change, prior to and for a short while after a politico-economic revolution. The vindication of its 'hoarseness of voice' —to use Brecht's phrase about some of his own writing in his poem "To Posterity"—the ultimate triumph and also eclipse of this art would lie in the aid it lent to introducing post-alienational conditions, where truth might be embodied effortlessly at a high plane by the specific resources of art, to assume a durable place beside the still aesthetically compelling works of antiquity.

If Marx and Engels assumed a certain neglect of the available potential for aesthetic specificity by much 'rebel' art, they believed that alienation ate all the more corrosively even into ambitious art which broadly corresponded to the attitudes, interests, or habits of thought of a modern ruling class. The term 'class equivalent' is especially useful in describing attributes of art which, whether unwittingly or lazily, take their impress from the dominant values fostered by a class having power: for the transference from model to receptive medium is the less labored and the more direct. The term 'class equivalent' originated with Georgij Plekhanov, the father of Russian Marxism, but Marx and Engels often discerned the phenomenon, describing in extended texts or in letters how an artist's stated or implied values were equivalent to aspects of the ideology of a social class. These connections were founded on explicit evidence in a work of art—never on mere reference to a writer's or artist's class of origin, which would have been reductive. When they discerned a socio-historical equivalent, how did they categorize it? Usually in one of these ways:

1. The work could be associated with the consciously-held, comprehensive world view of a broad historical class (see for example the texts on Aeschylus and Chateaubriand).

2. Even more broadly, the work could be associated with the hegemonic ideology of the era (Engels on Dante or on medieval poetry, Marx on German Reformation literature).

3. The work could more restrictively be attributed to a single political position (the equivalence of Heine or *Junges Deutschland* to a particular perception of German events).

The more narrow characterization was reserved usually—not surprisingly, either—for works that were relevant to recent national politics. The immediacy of the political ideology in art and literature also led to application of the major class categories 'bourgeois' and 'proletarian' more broadly. From the standpoint of changing social attitudes among artists, too, the politicized perception of the equivalents in recent works was justified. For artists in the nineteenth century were taking sides more, sympathized with a political party, or joined 'the party of Art.' The art for art's sake movement is not specifically mentioned by Marx or by Engels. Yet, they surely were aware of its conception. Indirectly, they disparaged it when they spoke of sophisticated egotistical art meant for a restricted circle. While Marx and Engels seem to have found *l'art pour l'art* hostile to the alienating conditions, they did not applaud its solution. If my interpretation is correct, they likened aesthetes such as Max Stirner to the Romantic movement, which they disapproved. If an either-or choice of the class affinities demonstrated by the anti-ideological aesthetes had to be made, undoubtedly Marx and Engels linked them more closely with the bourgeois than with proletarian values. The scorn stated by *l'art pour l'art* for the philistinism and class egotism of the bourgeoisie would not have been a sufficient counter-argument—which is only to recognize that the crucial choice in the Marxian philosophy of history was not between philistine accumulation and expertise, nor even between property and culture, but rather the choice had to be taken on a larger basis: one which might see property and philistinism and the cultural inheritance and contemporary art, chiefly organized for the benefit of a single one of the confronting sides. Ultimately the choice for any person lay between, on the one hand, the ruling class which jealously defended its power to own, to oppress, inherit, and exploit, and on the other hand, the most oppressed class, the working class, whose successful struggle for liberation would mean the abolition of class society and of alienation and, consequently, the full solution to the aspects of alienation which *l'art pour l'art* had cleverly but inadequately evaded, along with the solution of the misshaping oppression and exploitation endemic to class-divided societies through all recorded history.

However, while Marx and Engels made their ultimate contemporary value-choices in terms of the conflict of the bourgeoisie and proletariat, they often used a more particularized social categorization, and this also was true of their approach to class values in art. According to the artistic matter at hand, they might speak of the shopkeepers' literary representative, or of the involuted, class-contradictory ideas of a complex artist such as Goethe. On the whole their use of class analysis is sensitive and flexible, and it is oriented to the work of art. Nor should we look away from the fact that by no means did they make class values the main focus of their attention to art. Let us consider a case of their flexibility in applying the developed categories: the letter from Engels to Paul Ernst, dated June 5, 1890, in which Engels replies to this young Social-Democrat's propositions on the class nature of Scandinavian literature and of Ibsen in particular. Engels carefully distinguishes between the petty-bourgeoisie in Germany and in Norway—this same class in Norway, he argues, plays a far more positive historical role, which in turn contributes to the vitality of Scandinavian writing. Their methodology prevailed, not a blind application of dominant themes.

Historicist sensitivity is also evident in the observations of Marx and Engels on the category of the tragical. They apply the notion of tragedy to a drama about premature revolution (the *Sickingen* correspondence), but also to an ailing class regime that quixotically hopes to maintain its dignity (Marx's "Introduction to the Critique of Hegel's Philosophy of Right," 1843). These observations on tragedy, by the way, were never put forward by them in the trappings of a fully-developed theory. The ambiguity of its possible further development remains. The treatment of *Sickingen* suggests that tragical clash is inevitable when an epochal historical initiative met by practical class impossibility is turned back; another version of this impasse is seen in the tragicomedy of Quixote, where the initiative comes from the representative of a class whose dominance has passed. Further, the *Sickingen* discussion turns on an institution which readily defeats the prophetic impertinences of an individual; while the Quixote instance posits the values of two class institutions in conflict. If Marx and Engels had developed these discussions further, their unity might have become evident—but left as they were, we necessarily have questions which beg for answers. Among them: to what extent and how were these clashes compelled by objective history? To what extent, if at all, may the consciousness of individuals be thought capable of indeed transcending historical contexts (and thus give the 'tragical' awareness to historical conduct and the compelling necessity to the clash)? If the latter can occur, then the Marxian category of the tragical would lie not in epochal necessities which majestically conflict (Hegel's version), but in the defeat by institutionalized objectives of an individual challenge that points to a new era. In other words: the tragedy would not merely consist of two conflicting classes whose embodying protagonists clash (objective meshing of epochs of class history), instead tragedy would lie in the somewhat quixotic yet heroic 'vanguard' whose prescience and boldness to act expose it to personal destruction by representatives of the ruling class. Perhaps the ambiguity can be resolved along such lines.

But as the texts we have stand, much less than an aesthetic category of the tragical is presented—and the Eastern European Marxists, who would offer a comprehensive formulation from the insufficient arguments in Marx and Engels, while insensitively failing to deal with the further aesthetic problems, do a disservice. On the other hand, there are no grounds for accepting George Steiner's assertion in *The Death of Tragedy* (1961) that Marxian philosophy removes the basis for tragedy. For Marx's view of the clashes between epochal values, with humiliation and destruction awaiting those which arrive too early or depart too late, promises to remain relevant for the foreseeable future of socialist developments, as the statements in *The German Ideology* on the early phase of communism also suggest. Again, this argument was made by A. Lunacharsky, later the Commissioner of Education under Lenin, as early as 1908 (Steiner, by the way, credits Lunacharsky with just the opposite view, one supporting the 'death' of tragedy). It is true that some minor Soviet writers after World War II maintained the theory that socialist society was free of major conflicts, but this Panglossian attitude cannot be ranked beside the Marxian understanding of the social and aesthetic sources of tragedy.

To wind up this section, we may note that either of two Marxian emphases can be given to interpretation of the class conditioning of artistic values. In the more deterministic sense, this notion means that the expression of the work of art will conform to the ideology of a particular class, as imposed upon and mediated by the artist. A more comprehensive interpretation will find that the class conditioning of artistic values primarily occurs—or at least most profoundly occurs—where epochal class conflicts are depicted with lucid and deft control by artists who have an exceptional awareness of the historical framework and the dynamic of the tale they would tell. This more adequate, and more aesthetically understood, Marxian idea of the class determinates of major art brings us to the question of realism as an aesthetic category.

d. *The Problem of Realism*

By its standard of authentic portrayal of reality in art, Marxian aesthetic thought gains its chief verification of class-determined art in the narrower first sense discussed above. If art can render the true and determinate historical cross-section and dynamic of reality, then the departures from this capacity shall be known by the bias of their discrepancies.

The term 'realism' does not appear in any text by Marx. Yet, there is no doubt, after his comments on the Sue novel, the Lassalle play, and the great nineteenth-century novelists, that Marx agreed with the general conception formulated by Engels in his letters to Minna Kautsky and Margaret Harkness. Realism can be described as the artistic-cognitive value of an artwork. That their notion of the cognitive equivalent was broader than the overt ideological equivalent is shown in their discussion of Balzac. It baldly asserts that an artist can 'see,' i.e., perceive, more than even his own, vaunted ideological standpoint encourages. Undoubtedly, the freedom which is implied in the ability to embody cognitive equivalents will be tempered by certain fixed ideas about contemporary class virtues and failings. Yet, the narrower sense of class values is excluded from predominating in artistic cognition which can be called realism. Balzac's royalist leanings did not prevent him as a novelist from portraying contemporary French society with a breadth and acuity which offered a major indictment of royalist politics.

Whether a work achieved authentic realism was not to be judged, then, from the standpoint of 'progressive' or 'reactionary' class values that might be lodged in it, as such. Rather, such values, if present, were another although related issue. Authenticity of realism was to be achieved by, and judged by, the expression of a cognitive equivalent: specifically, the dominant and typical traits of socially conflicted life in a particular place and time. *Typicality* is thus a key consideration. An historically typical situation is at least partly unlike any previous historical moment, and it has to be bodied forth with freshness of character and event. This means individuality and specificity are an integral aspect of typicality. But with the appreciation of fidelity to detail goes a decisive attention to typical characteristics of life in a time and place. (The literary field, of course, provided the model for realism as an aesthetic category—Marx and Engels both turned to literature as their source of examples and their preference of all the arts. Their remarks on painting are few, but these suggest a similar standard for realism in painting: see Marx's comments on Rembrandt, or Engels' letter to Marx of May 20, 1857, admiring the portrait of Ariosto by Titian.) A guiding adjunct to their postulate of typicality is found in Marx's comment (*Capital*, vol. III) that history must be understood by expecting "many variations and gradations"—no single model for typicality may be advanced.

Realism was explicitly addressed and explored as a dominant theme of Marx and Engels; this does not mean they left no ambiguities in their approach, as we have it documented. Nor can we regard realism as their ultimate priority of concern in the arts, or, for that matter, as virtually their sole contribution to aesthetic thought—as various authors want to maintain. Among the lacunae left by their thought on realism: did Marx and Engels feel that typicality of both characters and circumstances must optimally appear in a realist work? Or could one have atypical characters in typical circumstances? And typical characters in atypical circumstances? Writing to Minna Kautsky in 1885, Engels stressed typicality of both characters and setting; but writing to M. Harkness in 1888, Engels seems to accept that typical figures can occur in rather exceptional circumstances, without leaving the category of realism. It might be possible to conclude that the norm of superior realism will be a fresh and specified typicality of both characters and setting; one might want to rank realist works in respect to their degree of typification.

Another area needing further study is that of the relation of an author's world view—the ideology—to the artistic-cognitive values of a work. In the Balzac instance, Marx and Engels found a complete discrepancy: on the one hand, the novels with their artistic-cognitive realism, and on the other, Balzac's ideological opinions as confirmed by non-art sources. However, a different relationship was found by Engels in Goethe's work, which sometimes was artistic-cognitive on a grand scale, and sometimes was merely ideological and inartistic. Goethe could be Olympian and philistine by turns. At the opposite remove from Balzac was Eugène Sue, whose work was entirely ideological; *The Mysteries of Paris* swallowed the world, its concreteness and typicality, and gave the reader only the writer's world view, with an opinionated fixity which obliterated nearly all sources in cognition. These three treatments by Marx and Engels may be taken to suggest the full scale of relations between world view and artistic cognition. There are numerous works of analysis which would further refine the scale.

How did they judge the worth of ideology in a work of art, in relation to the worth of artistic cognition? Marx and Engels rejected the ubiquity of a world view, as such, in a long work of fiction such as *The Mysteries of Paris* or, for that matter, in the play Lassalle had written. Engels advised Minna Kautsky in the letter earlier cited that it was better for the author's opinions to be hidden away; a reader might better draw his own conclusions about the cognitive representation. Fully-achieved works of art, they seemed to believe, will find means of avoiding the imposition of a discursive outlook on the public. This reluctance to admit ideology to a central place in artistic realism is complementary to their notion of a relative autonomy, or autotelicism, of the artistic medium—which provides a distinctive trait of artistic objects, and is realized only owing to their specific values and attributes. Ideology, as such, is not a trait distinctive to art.

A dynamic typicality, on the other hand, may be wholly expressed by the non-discursive means of mimetic art. We can still ask questions about aspects of the dynamic factor which are not clear in the texts we have. For instance, will a fully-achieved realism always put the dynamic emphasis on socially emerging situations and characters? Or is it reasonable to represent the dynamics of decay? The Engels letter to Harkness makes it definite that the classical texts of Marxian aesthetic thought are very far from laying down regulations for every eventuality. Harkness had emphasized a prolonged lapse of English workers from militancy. Engels responded with a question rather than a directive: "And how do I know whether you have not had very good reasons for contenting yourself, for once, with a picture of the passive side of working class life, reserving the active side for another work?"

e. 'Tendency' Writing

The artistic cognition of the typical and dynamic aspects of real life was thought to be not only better art but also better testimony on behalf of the socialist movement, than could be supplied by the artist's world view as such. However, the depiction of the socially-emergent forces of history was relevant to art in other modes than the realist medium alone with its special requirements.

When the artist consciously and overtly projected in art the idea of socialism as the emergent force of history, the source of the artistic aim might have been in direct cognition of reality or it might have been in ideology (and secondarily in cognitive inquiry): but the result, for art, was emphasis foremostly on world view, supported in its appeal by various artistically attractive qualities of the work, such as rhythm, irony, variation, etc., with confirming mimetic detail taking a subordinate place. The outcome of orienting world view to the projection of a vision of history, moreover, was to achieve an artistically more dynamic medium than ideological expression often could find. Realism was of course not in question. Instead, another dominant theme of Marx and Engels came to the fore: 'tendency' writing, the projection by essentially discursive yet poeticized means of an idea of history and of the attitudes, feelings, conflicts, etc., of the artistic personality (the author) about this idea. Obviously, the personal essay, the reflective or ironic poem, the expressionist play are more suitable mediums for 'tendency' writing than are the major realistic mediums, such as the novel and film.

'Tendency' writing, or tendentiousness, was a phenomenon of the 1840's in Germany, leading up to the 1848 Revolution, and, as such, Marx and Engels were much exposed to it, particularly in their youth. It has reappeared in many other contexts, often with other names being applied, such as 'committed writing' recently. This is perhaps the principal mode of 'rebel' art referred to in our discussion of alienation and disalienation. Its world view is guided by the hope for disalienation; it is generally an insistently politicized art, committed to depicting and provoking struggle against the established order that governs society.

As realism was described by Engels to Minna Kautsky, its goal is to embody the innate dialectics of social reality. It hints, if often broadly, at the trend or tendency of development active spontaneously in history. Repeatedly, Marx and Engels demarcated these latent cognitions of the tendency of social development from *l'art engagée*, with its explicit and didactic 'tendentiousness.' The latter was conceived from a consistent ideological position. Realism might be coherent in its underlying, peculiarly artistic cognition, or it might arise chaotically from a hodge-podge of conceptions, but the trend in events was latently not didactically given. While tendentious art has a positive goal to be gained, much realism emerges from a strong oppositional attitude towards contemporary social alienation which lacks a focused positive aspiration. The distinction can become blurred, art may be intensely realistic in part and prescriptive in part—Brecht's *Days of the Commune*, for instance. The point to be made is that art which expresses the dynamic of history may emphasize either a univocal worldview and a directed response from the audience, or an ambivalent and multivocal artistic realism which invites the audience to arrive at an opinion of the representation.

The above formulations may make it seem that Marx and Engels were not happy with 'tendency' writing—but this is by no means a general rule. For instance, the remarkable poet Heinrich Heine was a personal friend of Marx; Marx and Engels were delighted to have this political ally whose ideas, whose likes and dislikes stood out so forcefully in his verses. When in later years Heine became a backslider, they remonstrated him—not because he was tendentious in honor of elements of established religion and order, but because of his poor (opportunistic) choice of ideology he expressed. Similarly, the admired poet Ferdinand Freiligrath was welcomed by Marx and Engels to the party press. Marx commented to the poet, in a letter of February 29, 1860, that his tendentiousness had given splendid expression to the emergent social role of the proletariat, though Freiligrath had kept a distance between himself and the party with its politics and tactics; Marx emphasized the *Tendenz* inherent to all truthful creation. And in an article on the poet Georg Weerth of June 1883, Engels praised the way in which Weerth had been able to give prominence to the growing role of the working class in politics and society. Heine, Freiligrath, Weerth—these were 'tendency' poets, not realistic fiction writers; they spoke in their own voice, or in ballads, but with virtuoso intelligence and emotion and aesthetic elaboration and innovation of language. The expression of their artistic individuality offered the basis of a due autotelicism to the work, which the audience might confront with the 'distance' and 'freedom' that Marx mentioned in the *1844 Manuscripts* as necessary to the human creative attitude.

A word should be added to differentiate the position of Marx and Engels on *Tendenzkunst* from Lenin's idea of *partiinost*, a party-spirited literature. The distinction has been confused by Mikhail Lifshitz and other authors. Lenin makes a number of points in "Party Organization and Party Literature," the key text, which mostly centers on the party as a political vanguard and the artists who choose to become members of this organization. The question of discipline was very important for Lenin; for Marx it was not. Of course, Marx wished for an enduring understanding of artists for working people and their party, and he welcomed 'tendency' writing which with artistic brilliance pointed to the dynamic of history as he and this party understood it. However, Marx approached the artistic problems of depicting the tendency in social life very much as the artists themselves faced them—not with an invocation of discipline, but with concern for theme, character and setting, and the possible appearance of the personality of the artist in his work. It's not accidental, I believe, that no recorded opinion of Marx on the need or likelihood of a proletarian art is extant, nor can his opinion be extrapolated from available texts with any certainty; while Lenin, although reserved personally in his attitude, presided over the 'hothouse' emergence (as a party resolution of 1924 alluded to it) of a 'proletarian' group of party literary intellectuals; this was the nucleus which a few years after Lenin's death would take charge of what now is termed the Stalin era in Soviet literature.

f. *Expression of Fundamental Human Values in Art*

Seeing the question already arise at several preceding points as to where Marx and Engels actually placed the greater priority among various values relevant to the making of art, we can now try to settle the problem. We can most usefully introduce here Marx's famous thoughts on the enduring character of ancient Greek art.

What emerges from the question of priorities and that of the trans-historical character of Greek aesthetic achievements, if carefully synthesized, is another dominant theme: Marx's and Engels' idea of fundamental human values, which are equivalent to certain values expressed in art.

The fundamental human equivalents—those which are most trans-historical, most universally human—are only discussed by Marx directly in a single text, part of his analysis of Fleur de Marie, a prominent character in the Sue novel *Mysteries of Paris*. Fleur de Marie is said by Marx to have a vitality that goes beyond her bourgeois context and that forces its way through the clumsy moralizing imposed on the human subject-matter by Sue himself. Sue gives her example of *joie de vivre* something like a true embodiment.

Indirectly, Marx touches on fundamental human equivalents throughout his aesthetic thought. This is the necessary background to his all-out search for the means of social disalienation (which assumes a fundamental human potential). The unfailing appreciation Marx shows for the expression in art of sturdy and robust sensuality (also praised by Engels in his Weerth article), indomitable will, resilient enthusiasm, and passionate intellectual powers, is seen in his comments on the works of Aeschylus or Shakespeare, for example.

How then shall we read the praise for the enduring glory of Greek art? I believe it may be interpreted much in the way Max Raphael has suggested, as (a) recognition for the formal harmonious attributes achieved by ancient art. Yet, there seem to be two further criteria in the passage which Marx thought important to the enduring character of art. (b) By its own specific means art can express the whole significance of the society (Greek art was sustained by a system of living myth based in the specific mode and level of economic activity). (c) This art expressed the highest human values, and thereby offered a tremendous affirmation of humanity. It seems that Marx believed both the latter attributes were particularly suited to the art of a 'young' or naive civilization. It would be accurate to relate attribute (b) to artistic-cognitive value, and attribute (c) to fundamental human value. The cognitive and the fundamental human values mingle and are both dependent on attribute (a) which denotes the adequacy of form to the embodied values. And while we are making a full hierarchical scale, we should mention a progressive outlook as another criterion. Strictly speaking, this is an ideological equivalent. In the view of Marx and Engels, the criterion of progressive ideology cannot occur alone—for this value must be embodied with adequate formal expression, and moreover it is an expression of fundamental human value in another garb, as it were.

The hierarchy, or priority, of these enduring values was never deliberately settled by Marx or Engels; yet, as I indicated earlier, their aesthetic thought elaborates what we may accurately describe as a *Gehaltästhetik*, aesthetics oriented to content. Because 'form' was less important to them than 'content,' and in light of Marx's unwavering attachment to the Greek example and to the ideal of disalienated humanity, I believe the top priority among the enduring values, for Marx and Engels, should be recognized as the fundamentally human value embodied in art. As for the priority of ideological value and cognitive value over formal value, a number of examples demonstrate it. There is the explicit comment by Engels to Lassalle in the 1859 correspondence, where Engels says he approached the *Sickingen* play with the highest standards, "historical and aesthetic." Historical here means, of course, cognitive and ideological criteria, and aesthetic means formal; distinctly the latter standard is brought in secondarily. The parallel letter by Marx is similar.

We should not conclude from the foregoing that form was of no interest to them, or that they took artistic realization for granted. On the contrary—their criticism of *Sickingen* was in substance as much artistic as ideological; they were basically dissatisfied with Lassalle's artistic skills, their reason for accusing him of "Schillerizing" (a pun on the German word for describing), i.e., the use of 'mouthpiece' characters to utter the author's discursive thought, as well as in other ways substituting the orator's art for the craft of the artist. Nevertheless, readers may object that, in pursuing *Gehaltästhetik*, Marx and Engels did not display overmuch sensitivity to the specific problems of artistic form; they invoked these problems only cursorily, and without much interest. Driving this argument home, the reader may cite the fact that Lassalle's play strongly affected Marx and Engels although Lassalle, the lawyer and politician, was not a genuine artist. Engels was capable of sincerely praising the novels of M. Kautsky and M. Harkness which, while being mediocre works, now have some stature in the history of criticism due mainly to his admiration. Can we accept the above arguments, all of which have been made in print? Not finally.

The aesthetic sensibilities of Marx and Engels are more reliably judged by the passion and longevity of their responses to Shakespeare, Cervantes, Goethe, and Balzac; by the response of Engels to Ibsen and of Marx to the Greek dramatists—all in the original languages. We learn from Paul Lafargue's reminiscences that Marx also read and loved Pushkin, Gogol, and Shchedrin in the native Russian; Franz Mehring comments on his liking for Scott and Fielding. As for the specific charges of bad taste lodged against them, it should be noted that, in extending some praise to Lassalle, they wanted to soften the blow of essentially severe criticisms, and Lassalle was their friend. Moreover, some of the praise was merited by the newness of Lassalle's project, and this applies also to Engels on Harkness and Kautsky. Surely, there is no shortage of serious critical thought extended to the novelty of works which, in their other dimensions, are perishable!

Let us suppose that Georg Büchner's drama *Danton's Death* had been known to them (it was not critically 'discovered' until half a century later): Marx and Engels would have had an innovating text worthy in its formal values as much as in its ideological, cognitive and fundamentally human values of their most discriminating analysis. Alas, it was not to be. The authors with world views nearest to their own did not, on the whole, rise to the highest artistic challenge, or at least they did not in drama or long fiction which have been the eminent fields of realism. This left Marx and Engels with only older works to enjoy on a comprehensive scale of the enduring artistic values, and enjoy such works as they certainly did. Marx himself wanted to write a drama about the Roman Gracchi, a revolutionary episode from the ancient world, we are told by Lafargue. In short, Marx and Engels took their fullest aesthetic pleasure where they could, and discussed the developing social and politically-sympathetic drama and novel where they could.

Even with the merited recognition of their aesthetic responsiveness, however, we must conclude that they directed more attention to problems of *Gehaltästhetik* than to developing a formal interpretation. And they did regard form—which I take to be the primary constituent attribute of any work of art—in an instrumental fashion. That is to say, they often wrote as though it were a transparent if necessary value, which, if competently disposed, would permit the content (which had its own problems) to shine brightly through. On occasion—writing about style, or on Lassalle's drama—they did treat form as a translucent value, that is, with its compositional attributes or failings always apparent to the responding public or to critical analysis. Surely their concern for some novel problems of *Gehaltästhetik* took a toll on the equitably balanced approach we might have hoped from them. But the cost is offset, in a way, by their recurrent concern for the fundamentally human value, which they moreover saw to direct the attention of everyone attuned to aesthetic realization back onto the ultimate source of both present and potential harmonious formal value: that is to say, back onto the alienation and disalienation of the human species, in its basic characteristics and its astonishing, irrepressible desire for freedom and fulfillment.

A final word must be said on a point suggested above: the high regard that Marx and Engels had for originality, not only in the artistic-cognitive and ideological dimension, but also and strikingly in the stylistic dimension. This begins early: in the letter on style from Engels to W. Gräber, and in Marx's response to the Prussian censorship. It is emphasized in the *Communist Manifesto* which speaks of communism as "an association, in which the free development of each is the condition for the free development of all," a definition echoed in *Capital* where communism is termed "a higher type of society whose fundamental principle is the full and free development of every individual." The vision of the future era, as earlier discussed, includes the prospect of every person realizing his or her specific artistic aptitudes, which all will command. In short, it is communism alone that could bring out individual abilities and enable them to mature among the great majority whose lives had been stunted in previous societies. It is communism alone that could generate the best and most original results of aesthetic activity and the freest expressions of genius.

Yet, if individual style was among the chief values that they attributed to artistic achievement, I do not see how it may be introduced among the dominant themes—at least, on the terms set out for presenting the other dominant themes. Marx and Engels simply did not develop their thought on it as an aesthetic category. They did not specifically indicate how the presence of originality affects the whole of the aesthetic work, how it interrelates with the remaining chief values. I would not care to speculate about their thought in this matter, with so little to go on. Other areas of the aesthetic thought of Marx and Engels can be recognized, reconstructed, interpolated and extrapolated. But here, the importance—and the lacunae—can only be acknowledged.

Inquiry and study as to the sources contributing to the aesthetic thought of Marx and Engels has begun. To this date, it has not been exhaustive.

In part for this reason, the scholars who address themselves to Marxian aesthetic thought have often accepted misstatements, or have relied on their own preconceptions; this in turn has led to misinterpretations, of three kinds. (a) One approach, typified by Lifshitz, almost wholly overlooks the influence of the history of aesthetics on the two men—that is to say, the idiogenetic sources of their aesthetic thought. Another mistaken approach, (b) that of Jezuitow and others, sees the development of the ideas of Marx and Engels on art as an 'ontogenetic' repetition of the 'philogenetic' pattern of change in German and European aesthetics from the late Enlightenment to Hegel. This is at least a quasi-idiogenetic interpretation in part, although schematized beyond the point of usefulness; another such is (c) that of Fridlender among others, who takes the dictum from Lenin that Marxism's primary sources are the German classical philosophy, the English political economy, and the French utopian socialism, and applies this schema indiscriminately.

These hasty or confused approaches to the available evidence will not do. On the one hand, it is impossible to doubt the great importance which earlier aesthetic thought had for Marx and Engels; on the other hand, it must be patiently examined, to understand the specific extent and way in which this heritage was grasped by Marxian thought. Thorough empirical study is called for—and has been supplied, in great part, by a doctoral dissertation on the period from the Enlightenment through Schiller to Hegel by Stanislav Pazura ("Marks a klasyczna estetyka niemiecka," Warsaw, 1967). What is the evidence which Pazura turns up, and how should it be interpreted?

The parallels between the conceptions of Marx and those of German aesthetics in this period are prominent. In the letters of 1837 from Marx to his father and his reading excerpts to 1842 (*MEGA*, pp. 115-118) we can observe his intensive reading of the literature on aesthetics; indeed, Marx's knowledge of it far surpasses what was to be expected of a philosophy student at the time. And Engels' early writings convince us he had poured over the aesthetics of the 'Young Germany' movement, which introduced him to the ideas of Lessing, Goethe, and Schiller. We can also find evidence that Marx returned at various times—1851-52, 1857, 1874—to study the aesthetic heritage. There must have been many other occasions when Engels or Marx directly consulted the aesthetic tradition. This is not the place to itemize what is definitely known of their reading. But we may sketch in a general way how the dominant themes in their aesthetic thought compare with the 'background' in their time.

This brings us to German classical aesthetics. To Hegel, of course. Yet, not only to Hegel as its 'summit,' as some have argued, but also to the stimulus of many earlier figures and many different modes. The admiration for Greek culture stems from Winckelmann. And an entire line in German philosophy points to the question of alienation. The fragmentation of modern life contrasted with the ideal of the rich, harmonious personality was discussed by Winckelmann, Kant, Schiller, and lesser writers (e.g., K. Heydenreich, M. Herz). Many authors believed that art could play the chief role in bringing about humanity's inner integration and full adaptation to the social world. Indeed, an excessive hope was often invested in art during this time in Germany. Even the most general speculative texts of the period sometimes contained an aesthetic anthropology: e.g., Fichte's Letters of 1794 ("Ueber Geist und Buchstab in der Philosophie"), or the anonymous essay "Das älteste System-Program des deutschen Idealismus" (1796, attributed by Cassirer to Hölderlin, by Walzel to F. Schlegel, by Allwohn and Zeltner to Schelling, and even to Hegel—see A. Nivelle, *Les Theories esthétiques en Allemagne de Baumgarten à Kant*, 1955). Much was also written on the dispiriting advances of alienation in art. For example, G. Forster's "Die Kunst und das Zeitalter," *Thalia*, no. 9, 1789; Fichte, *op.cit.*; A.W. Schlegel, Marx's teacher, "Briefe über Poesie, Silbenmass und Sprache," *Horen*, 1795; and finally, Hegel (his notion of the *Zerfallen der Kunst*, the decadence of art). Marx's contemporary, F.T. Vischer, continues this more or less Rousseauean trend, where he denounces the sterile, authoritarian, bureaucratic apparatus of capitalist society which destroys beauty and particularly degrades the aesthetic level of the working population (*Aesthetik*, 1846-57). What about the background to Marx's and Engels' treatment of the genesis of aesthetic sensibility and art in relation to labor? This is discussed earlier by A.W. Schlegel, who accorded a primordial role to rhythm which he traced to the natural and social relations of humanity in the material world. Schlegel also suggested that the artist-specialist was unknown in primitive society, and that the autonomization of art would have occurred at a later time. Marx undoubtedly knew Schiller's writing on this topic. Schiller had demarcated the senses of animals from a strictly human sensibility; the latter, more detached from an immersing reality, could become the basis of a *freie Ideenfolge* and the emergence of a *Spieltrieb* which, imparting to human activity and production a specificity of form, at last gave rise to the *ästhetischer Schein*. What of the attributes of the aesthetic object and aesthetic experience? Marx's thought incorporates Kant's *freies Spiel der Seelenkräfte*. However, the solution to this problem in respect to the subject/object relationship—the notion of the harmony of the aesthetic object corresponding to the integral and autotelic character of the aesthetic experience—was indicated by Heydenreich, Herz, and Schiller. And it was a common-enough solution: witness K. Chr. F. Krause's *Abriss der Aesthetik* (1837). There is no question that the *1844 Manuscripts* use notions and even phrasings identical with those of Feuerbach in *The Essence of Christianity* (1841). What about the emphasis on *Gehaltästhetik*? Major attention to 'content' extends from Schiller through Hegel to the young Vischer, and, of course, to *Junges Deutschland*. And Marx and Engels stood with the 'Young Germany' movement in rejecting Hegel's expectation of a permanent decline of art, while from the same source they learned to understand and appreciate a politically committed art. On the other hand, from Vischer (*Aesthetik*) they could gain the notion that beauty is possessed of its own tendency, contained in the art work. Hegel's immediate influence is especially felt in the references by Marx to the comic and tragic, to the enduring glory of Greek art, and to the typical, a concept at the center of the realism of Marx and Engels. Thus, German classical aesthetics may be considered the primary source of their aesthetic thought.

Yet, we should notice that other European traditions of thought were available. Notions of alienation and disalienation in the writings of Rousseau and the French utopian Socialists could easily haved influenced the thinking of Marx and Engels. Diderot, too, had located the genesis of art in the work processes; the prevailing German notion of realism which centered on the principle of *im Allgemeinen (das Besondere) das Einzelene*, was profoundly modified by ideas of the hero typifying a social situation (Diderot and Lessing), by the prefaces Balzac wrote to his novels, by the literary and artistic movement in the 1840's and 1850's—G. Sand, Courbet, Champfleury, such English novelists as Dickens and Thackeray. At a later date, the controversy over Zola and the naturalist novel provides a setting for Engels' letters on realism; and his emphasis on a realistic 'truth of detail' cannot be divorced from his concern for a typicality of character and situation, directed against the naturalist enthusiasts—for example, his letter of December 13, 1883 to Laura Lafargue, where Engels declares the "revolutionary dialectics" of Balzac had taught him more about the history of France in 1815-48 than had the history books. As for class interpretation of art, the first, however tentative and faulty, stems from Mme. de Staël and the French *doctrinaires* (Guizot, Ballanche, de Barante). This is a lengthy account of resources and sources, and I must add that Marx, who was astonishingly erudite, would surely have looked behind the immediately available aesthetic tradition—much as he learned from it—to make the ideas of Plato, Aristotle, and Dürer a part of his intellectual preparation. On the other hand, he undoubtedly did not read all the authors cited above. Many of the ideas were in general intellectual circulation; he must have run across them in a number of ways.

That is the idiogenetic background to Marxian aesthetics. We have seen that this area of their work cannot be interpreted apart from an understanding of their general world view or philosophy. What were, in turn, the main non-aesthetic influences on the thought of Marx and Engels? Hegel's general philosophy helped indirectly shape the body of dominant themes, observations, and remarks; yet, despite the importance to them of such notions as *versinnlichter Geist, Weltzustand, das Typische,* the central formative influence simply cannot be awarded to Hegel alone. No less significant was the great philosophical movement toward an historicist perspective—commencing at the start of the eighteenth century with Vico, Montesquieu and Rousseau, Winckelmann and Herder, through the French *doctrinaires* and Hegel's philosophy of history to the English economists and French historians. Another non-aesthetic influence was the idea of modern progress, which often brimmed with utopian enthusiasms. The revolutionary 1770's furthered this social and political ideology which evolved to combine the thirst for justice and the desire for community with a projection of better times either backwards to a dim past or forward to a distant future. The *1844 Manuscripts* echo the sigh for a 'noble savage' in a primeval unalienated past. Closely related was the idea of an integrated harmony between man and society in ancient Greece. Here Marx followed Winckelmann, Hölderlin, Hegel, and others. But for Marx the idea of better human conditions was chiefly oriented to the future—and here he and Engels stood in the tradition of Condorcet, Fichte, such eighteenth-century utopians as Morelly or Don Deschamp, and the industrial-utopians Saint Simon and Robert Owen.

The influence of the Romantic School merits a special discussion. Scholars have conclusively demonstrated that Marx and Engels independently started out as followers of this movement, only to reject it under Hegel's influence, as others also did. No German Romantic could cope with the devastating, unanswerable shafts launched by Hegel commencing with *The Phenomenology of Spirit.* Thus Marx decided, with Bruno Bauer, also active in Young Hegelian circles, to write a sardonic attack on Romantic art. It had become Marx's conviction that Romanticism was in league with religious art and its attendant ideology which at that time were his major targets for attack. This insensitivity to the aesthetic values of the Middle Ages was reinforced by his reading of De Brosses, Grund, Ruhmor and others. He echoed their words about the alleged barbarism of Gothic style. The same hostility motivated Marx's and Engels' hard words against Carlyle in 1850. The contrast to the deformed sickly medieval art was the antique art of Greece, which Marx pronounced healthy and normal and never ceased to admire as the ideal of beauty. In later letters to Engels, Marx sarcastically ridiculed the style of Chateaubriand as a concatenation of vanity and false profundity, Byzantine exaggeration and polite sentimentalism. However, it has to be noted that Chateaubriand's characteristics are not a summation of the Romantic School. That movement also contained Byron and Shelley, for whom Marx and Engels held great respect. There is little doubt that they made a distinction between 'Philistine' Romanticism and a plebeian and folklore-oriented Romanticism. Also, with the passing of years, they found more to value in medieval art and craftsmanship. During the very days that he corrected proof on *Capital,* Marx passed his spare hours enjoying the 'dreams, frenzy, illusions' of the Spanish Catholic playwright Calderon. Their interest was caught by the brilliant inventions of German Romantics like Chamisso and E.T.A. Hoffmann (as pointed out earlier, they placed great value in individuality of style in art). In sum—Marx and Engels fought tenaciously against the *romantische Schule* in philosophy, ideology, and aesthetics, against Schelling and Solger. In the context of the intellectual currents of the early 1840's, they certainly were anti-Romantics. However, in a broader sense, Marx and Engels were cradled by Romanticism. This movement suffused all sides of the controversies of the day; it was the matrix in which antinomies were framed. How does the influence appear? It can be discovered in the way they structured questions about: (a) the egotistical freedom of the artist vs. his responsibility to nation, society, and humanity; (b) the artist as a lonely virtuoso of beauty or perhaps an acolyte of eternal truth vs. his revolutionary obligation or commitment; (c) a specifically aesthetic function of art vs. cognitive and moral functions; (d) unbridled individualist fantasy vs. the obedience of art to definite laws of the spirit or of nature; (e) *aut delectare aut prodesse*.‡ It is obvious that Marx and Engels could not be content with the typical manner of posing questions at that time—but it was another matter to shake off entirely the effects of this mode of antinomy.

This has been the catalogue of what Marx and Engels accepted from their background and critically assimilated into their intellectual system. What they rejected is also important, and a sketch of their negative choices is instructive. Directly or indirectly, Marx and Engels attacked the objective idealism of Krause, Weisse, and Hegel, and the subjective idealism of Kant, Fichte, the *romantische Schule*. They rejected the art for art's sake doctrine, and equally, or nearly so, they opposed a banal didacticism. While respecting the value of form, they opposed formalism. They did not disclaim the presence of a natural impulsion underlying aesthetic experience, but they did not agree with the naturalistic notion that a specific aesthetic instinct was common both to man and other animals.

VI. *Conclusion*

The panorama of the indirect and the immediate, the possible and the explicit sources and resources is immense. A reader could easily but too hastily conclude that Marx and Engels themselves must have, in their own right, contributed little or nothing to the history of aesthetic thought. Indeed, the attempt has been made by a number of Western scholars on the subject to compress most of their concepts into Hegel and the French realist doctrine of the 1850's. Among some Soviet scholars a comparable tendency more or less identifies Marxian thought with the views of Belinsky or Chernyshevsky. Either way, an impermissibly narrow and selective use of data occurs.

I have tried here to reconstruct Marxian aesthetic thought in its integrity, yet with a minimum recourse to extrapolation, accepting and mindful of the limits of using an outline approach, one which separates the texts into a documentary entity apart.

‡ To enjoy, to learn.

What emerges from this attempt at interpretation? I do not find the entire Marxian aesthetic contribution reducible to the sum of its sources; nor do I find its parts interchangeable with other, parallel formulations. What does this mean for Marx's and Engels' notion of alienation and disalienation? Well, they formulated this problem in an entirely new way, and Marx's philosophy of history is the ultimate reason for its originality. What else is new in this approach? Marx and Engels contributed to a new understanding of the priorities among the values embodied by art. They found a new solution to the old dilemma which saw art at once dying out and providing hope and comfort to a presently suffering humanity. The achievement of *homo aestheticus* could be anticipated, Marx thought, but a radical socio-political change in the situation of the species would be required. In this particular sense, the artist had to make a choice. Would he bemuse himself in an ivory tower, or participate in revolutionary progress by accepting its vicissitudes? Tendentiousness acquires a new meaning in Marx and Engels, not found among their forerunners. *Tendenz* is recast in the context of the Marxian world view, and historical reality itself is described as 'tendentious.' And this modifies the question of realism. The Hegelian notion of a type depicted in specific circumstances (*ein dieser*) is accepted, but they introduce to realism an awareness of the socially emergent elements. Ideology here comes to be considered a component of artistic choice and discrimination. The nature of a profound and true tendentiousness is to further refine and shape the artistic-cognitive values united within the aesthetic entity. Or again, the genesis of aesthetic sensibility is newly interpreted by reference to dialectical and historical materialism. And the transformation of *homo faber* into *homo ludens* is seen as a profoundly social phenomenon, so much so that even the process of art's autonomization has to be seen historically. The dominant theme of class equivalents of art, we know, has been accepted universally as a Marxian emphasis; and while the class dimension of art had been observed earlier, Marx and Engels were the first ones to see it in its proper dimension and to explore the complexities. In conclusion, I believe that it is now apparent that the dominant themes of Marx and Engels presented new issues for nineteenth-century aesthetics.

Needless to say, they could not lift themselves above the horizon of their time which defined the decisive issues for them. In this sense, their sympathy for realism is symptomatic—and yet, I must add that, nowhere in their work did Marx and

Engels declare themselves against any alternative methods and solutions for art.

From another aspect, too, they were unable to deal with all the fundamental problems of aesthetics we would like to see treated. They were not professionals in the field. Also, and this is more basic, they adopted a specific and selective approach to the problems of art. From this standpoint, the omissions or lacunae we find among their aesthetic ideas are as revealing as the contributions we see to have originated with them.

Accordingly, to suggest that Marx and Engels provided a rounded, balanced aesthetic theory would be incorrect. On the other hand, to dismiss their ideas as fortuitous or incidental speculations, or as utterances of mere taste and preference, would be just as irresponsible. I think that the reconstruction demonstrates how these aesthetic ideas have an internal coherence, not disrupted by any serious inconsistency. With a well-developed philosophy centering on several dominant themes, the ideas are addressed to problems that are thought to rank among the most significant and fundamental according to all traditional aesthetic treatises up to today.

I want to be clear on this point. The body of the aesthetic thought of Marx and Engels is not all-encompassing, and ostensibly it centers on literary examples. No final or complete system is offered. However, the contribution which an aesthetic approach makes eludes definition by such a test. A proper standard would be the originality of the contribution in its own time, and its influence on theory, criticism, and even artistic creativity in the future. By this test, the aesthetic ideas of Marx and Engels have historical and theoretical importance.

ORIGINS AND TRAITS OF THE AESTHETIC SENSIBILITY
ORIGINS AND TRAITS OF THE AESTHETIC SENSIBILITY

The animal is immediately identical with its life-activity. It does not distinguish itself from it. It is *its life-activity.* Man makes his life-activity itself the object of his will and of his consciousness. He has conscious life-activity. It is not a determination with which he directly merges. Conscious life-activity directly distinguishes man from animal life-activity...

Man (like the animal) lives on inorganic nature; and the more universal man is compared with an animal, the more universal is the sphere of inorganic nature on which he lives. Just as plants, animals, stones, air, light, etc., constitute a part of human consciousness in the realm of theory, partly as objects of natural science, partly as objects of art—his spiritual inorganic nature, spiritual nourishment which he must first prepare to make it palatable and digestible—so too in the realm of practice they constitute a part of human life and human activity...

In creating an *objective world* by his practical activity, in *working-up* inorganic nature, man proves himself a conscious species being, i.e., a being that treats the species as its own essential being, or that treats itself as a species being. Admittedly animals also produce. They build themselves nests and dwellings, like the bees, beavers, ants, etc. But an animal only produces what it immediately needs for itself or its young. It produces one-sidedly, while man produces universally. It produces only under the dominion of immediate physical need, while man produces even when he is free from physical need and only truly produces in freedom therefrom. An animal produces only itself, while man reproduces the whole of nature. An animal's product belongs immediately to its physical body, while man freely confronts his product. An animal forms things in accordance with the measure and the need of the species to which it belongs, while man knows how to produce in accordance with the measure of every species and knows how to apply everywhere the inherent measure to the object. Man, therefore, also forms things in accordance with the laws of beauty...

Just as music alone awakens in man the sense of music, and just as the most beautiful music conveys no meaning to the unmusical ear—is no object for it, because my object can only be the confirmation of one of my essential powers and can therefore only be so for me as my essential power exists for itself as a subjective capacity, because the meaning of an object for me goes only so far as *my* senses go (has only sense for a meaning corresponding to that object)—for this reason the *senses* of the social man are *other* senses than those of the non-social man. Only through the objectively unfolded richness of man's essential being is the richness of subjective *human* sensibility (a musical ear, an eye for beauty of form—in short, *senses* capable of human gratifications, senses confirming themselves as essential powers of *man*) either cultivated or brought into being. For not only the five senses but also the so-called mental senses—the practical senses (will, love, etc.)—in a word, *human* sense—the humanness of the senses—comes to be by virtue of its object, by virtue of *humanized* nature. The *forming* of the five senses is a labor of the entire history of the world down to the present.

The *sense* caught up in crude practical need has only a *restricted* sense. For the starving man, it is not the human form of food that exists, but only its abstract being as food; it could just as well be there in its crudest form, and it would be impossible to say wherein this feeding-activity differs from that of *animals*. The care-burdened man in need has no sense for the finest play; the dealer in minerals sees only the mercantile value but not the beauty and the unique nature of the mineral: he has no mineralogical sense. Thus, the objectification of the human essence both in its theoretical and practical aspects is required to make man's *sense human*, as well as to create the *human sense* corresponding to the entire wealth of human and natural substance.

The nations which are still dazzled by the sensuous splendor of precious metals and are, therefore, still fetish-worshippers of metal money are not yet fully developed money-nations.

MARX, from: *A Contribution to the Critique of Political Economy* (1859)

The great importance of metals in general in the direct process of production is due to the part they play as instrument of production. Apart from their scarcity, the great softness of gold and silver as compared with iron and even copper (in the hardened state in which it was used by the ancients), makes them unfit for that application and deprives them, therefore, to a great extent, of that property on which the use-value of metals is generally based. Useless as they are in the direct process of production, they are easily dispensed with as means of existence, as articles of consumption. For that reason any desired quantity of them may be absorbed by the social process of circulation without disturbing the processes of direct production and consumption. Their individual use-value does not come in conflict with their economic function. Furthermore, gold and silver are not only negatively superfluous, i.e. dispensable articles, but their aesthetic properties make them the natural material of luxury, ornamentation, splendor, festive occasions, in short, the positive form of abundance and wealth. They appear, in a way, as spontaneous light brought out from the underground world, since silver reflects all rays of light in their original combination, and gold only the color of highest intensity, viz. red light. The sensation of color is, generally speaking, the most popular form of aesthetic sense. The etymological connection between the names of the precious metals, and the relations of colors, in the different Indo-Germanic languages has been established by Jacob Grimm (see his *History of the German Language*)...

Suppose we have a commodity whose use-value is that of a diamond. We cannot tell by looking at the diamond that it is a commodity. When it serves as a use-value, aesthetic or mechanical, on the breast of a harlot or in the hand of a glasscutter, it is a diamond and not a commodity.

MARX, from: *Capital* (1867)

First of all, labor is a process between man and nature. In this process man mediates, regulates and controls his material interchange with nature by means of his own activity. Confronting the materiality of nature, he is himself a force of nature. With the natural forces of his body, his arms and legs and head and hand, he acts to appropriate the materiality of nature in a form useful to his life. Thus acting upon nature outside of him, and changing it, he changes his own nature also. The potentials that slumber within his nature are developed; and he compels the play of these forces to do his bidding. We do not here refer to the initial and instinctual forms of labor, as found among animals. The situation whereby the laborer appears in the commodity market as the seller of his own labor-power is at an immeasurable remove from the stage at which human labor had still to cast off its first and instinctual form. We are positing labor of a form that is exclusively characteristic of *man*. The operations carried out by a spider resemble those of a weaver, and many a human architect is put to shame by the bee in the construction of its wax cells. However, the poorest architect is categorically distinguished from the best of bees by the fact that before he builds a cell in wax, he has built it in his head. The result achieved at the end of a labor process was already present at its commencement, in the *imagination of the worker, in its ideal form.* More than merely working an *alteration* in the form of nature, he also *knowingly works his own purposes into* nature; and these purposes are the law determining the ways and means of his activity, so that his will must be adjusted to them. Nor is this adjustment a fleeting act. Both the exertion of the laboring organs and the *purposeful* will, evident as *attentiveness,* are required during the entirety of the work. The more so, the less that the innate content of the work and the ways and means of its realization are attractive to the worker; the less, therefore, that he enjoys the work as a play of his own physical and psychic powers.

ENGELS, from: *The Part Played by Labor in the Transition From Ape to Man* (1876)

Labor is the source of all wealth, the political economists assert. It is this, next to nature, which supplies it with the material that it converts into wealth. But it is even infinitely more than this. Labor is the prime basic condition for all human existence, and this to such an extent that, in a sense, we have to say that labor created man himself....

Many monkeys use their hands to build nests for themselves in the trees or even, like the chimpanzee, to construct roofs between the branches for protection against the weather. With their hands they seize hold of clubs to defend themselves against enemies, or bombard the latter with fruits and stones. In captivity, they carry out with their hands a number of simple operations copied from human beings. But it is just here that one sees how great is the distance between the undeveloped hand of even the most anthropoid of apes and the human hand that has been highly perfected by the labor of hundreds of thousands of years. The number and general arrangement of the bones and muscles are the same in both; but the hand of the lowest savage can perform hundreds of operations that no monkey's hand can imitate. No simian hand has ever fashioned even the crudest of stone knives.

At first, therefore, the operations for which our ancestors

gradually learned to adapt their hands during the many thousands of years of transition from ape to man could have been only very simple. The lowest savages, even those in whom a regression to a more animal-like condition with a simultaneous physical degeneration can be assumed to have occurred, are nevertheless far superior to these transitional beings. Before the first flint was fashioned into a knife by human hands, a period of time may have elapsed in comparison with which the historical period known to us appears insignificant, but the decisive step was taken: *the hand had become free* and could henceforth attain ever greater dexterity and skill, and the greater flexibility thus acquired was inherited and increased from generation to generation.

Thus the hand is not only the organ of labor, *it is also the product of labor*. Only by labor, by adaptation to ever new operations, by inheritance of the thus acquired special development of muscles, ligaments and, over longer periods of time, bones as well, and by the ever-renewed employment of this inherited finesse in new, more and more complicated operations, has the human hand attained the high degree of perfection that has enabled it to conjure into being the paintings of a Raphael, the statues of a Thorwaldsen, the music of a Paganini....

First labor, after it and then with it, speech—these were the two most essential stimuli under the influence of which the brain of the ape gradually changed into that of man, which for all its similarity is far larger and more perfect. Hand in hand with the development of the brain went the developement of its most immediate instruments—the sense organs. Just as the gradual development of speech is necessarily accompanied by a corresponding refinement of the organ of hearing, so the development of the brain as a whole is accompanied by a refinement of all the senses. The eagle sees much farther than man, but the human eye sees considerably more things than does the eye of the eagle. The dog has a far keener sense of smell than man, but it does not distinguish a hundredth part of the odors that for man are definite signs of denoting different things. And the sense of touch, which the ape hardly possesses in its crudest initial form, has been developed only side by side with the development of the human hand itself, through the medium of labor....

By the cooperation of hands, organs of speech and brain, not only in each individual but also in society, human beings became capable of executing more and more complicated operations, and of setting for themselves and achieving higher and higher aims. With each generation labor itself became different, more perfect, more diversified. Agriculture was added to hunting and cattle raising; then spinning, weaving, metalworking, pottery and navigation. Along with trade and industry, art and science finally appeared. Nations and states developed from tribes. Law and politics arose, and with them the fantastic mirror image of human things in the human mind: religion. In the face of all these creations, which appeared in the first place as products of the mind and which seemed to dominate human societies, the more modest productions of the working hand retreated into the background, the more so since the mind that planned the labor already at a very early stage of development of society (for example, already in the primitive family) was able to have the labor that had been planned carried out by other hands than its own. All merit for the swift advance of civilization was ascribed to the mind, to the development and activity of the brain. Men became accustomed to explaining their actions from their thoughts instead of from their needs (which in any case are reflected, come to consciousness in the mind)—and so there arose in the course of time that idealistic outlook on the world which, especially since the end of the ancient world, has dominated men's minds. It still rules them to such a degree that even the most materialistic natural scientists of the Darwinian school are still unable to form any clear idea of the origin of man, because under this ideological influence they do not recognize the part that has been played by labor.

CAPITALIST ALIENATION AND THE WARPING OF AESTHETIC VALUES

MARX, from: "Remarks on the New Instructions to the Prussian Censors" (1842)

The law permits me to write; it asks only that I write in a style other than *my own*! I am allowed to show the face of my mind, but, first, I must give it a *prescribed expression*! Where is the man of honor who would not turn crimson at this imposition, who would not prefer to hide his head under his toga? At least, the toga hints that it may conceal the head of a Jupiter underneath. Prescribed expressions mean only *bonne mine à mauvais jeu.*

You admire nature's enchanting multiplicity, its inexhaustible richness. You do not demand that the rose smell like the violet; and yet, the mind, which is richest of all, is to be allowed to exist in but a *single* mode? I am inclined to humoristic writing, but the law bids me be serious. My style is bold; but the law orders moderation. The sole permissible color of freedom is *gray on gray.* An inexhaustible play of colors glitters from each dewdrop on which the sun shines; and yet the mind's sun is to engender but one color, the *official color,* no matter how many individuals or which objects may be refracted! *Brightness* and *light* is the essential form of the mind, and you say that its only suitable manifestation is the *shadow* of it.

It is to be dressed only in black, although among flowers there is no black. The essence of mind is *always truth itself:* and what do you make of its essence? *Moderation.* Only a bedraggled beggar is modest, Goethe said; a bedraggled beggar, is that what you want to make out of the mind? Or is moderation to be the moderation of genius, as Schiller says? Then start by transforming each of your citizens, and your censors most of all, into geniuses. Indeed, the moderation of genius does not consist of the use of a cultivated language without accent or dialect; it lies rather in speaking the accent of the matter and the dialect of its essence. It lies in forgetting about moderation and immoderation and getting to the core of things. The underlying moderation of the mind lies in reason, that universal liberality which is related to *every nature* according to *its essential character. . . .*

Are we to understand quite simply that *truth* is what *the government ordains*? Is the *investigation* of truth deemed superfluous and inappropriate, and yet, *because* of *etiquette,* as a third aspect that cannot quite be dismissed? Evidently so. For investigation is regarded categorically as *opposed* to truth; therefore, it appears with the suspiciously official patina of seriousness and moderation which a layman is supposed to display before a priest. Governmental rationale is the sole rationality in the state. Concessions will of course be made to other reasoning and idle talk under certain circumstances; but by the same token, they will in turn assume a consciousness of concession and have no real authority—being modest and subservient, serious and boring. It was Voltaire who said: *tous les genres sont bons excepté le genre ennuyeux* [all genres are good but the boring genre], and here the boring genre becomes the only one as we can see from *Die Verhandlungen der Rheinischen Landstände* [*The Proceedings of the Rheinish States*]. Why not rather use the good old German Holy Office style? Freely shall you write, but let every word be a genuflection toward the liberal censor who approves your modest, serious good judgment. Be sure that you do not lose a consciousness of humility!

MARX, from: "Debating the Freedom of the Press" (1842)

At first it is startling to find *freedom of the press* subsumed under *freedom of doing business*. Yet, we must not condemn the views of the speaker out of hand. *Rembrandt* painted the Mother of God as a Dutch Peasant woman, and why should not our speaker paint freedom in an image that is immediate and familiar to him?...

To defend or even understand the freedom of a domain, I must grasp its essential character rather than its extrinsic connections. But is a press true to its own character, does it behave in accord with the nobility of its nature, *is the press free*, when it demeans itself and becomes a *business*? A writer must of course earn a living to exist and be able to write, but he must in no sense exist and write so as to earn a living.

When Beranger* sings:

Je ne vis, que pour faire des chansons,
Si vous m'otez ma place, Monseigneur,
Je ferai des chansons pour vivre,

(I only live to make my songs,
If you rob me of my place, Monseigneur,
I will make songs in order to live,)

there is an ironic avowal in this threat: the poet falls from his domain, as soon as his poetry becomes but a means.

* Pierre-Jean de Beranger (1780-1857), popular French songwriter.

In no sense does the writer regard his works as a *means*. They are *ends in themselves*; so little are they means for him and others that, when necessary, he sacrifices *his* existence to *theirs*, and like the preacher of religion, though in another way, he takes as his principle: "God is to be obeyed before men." He himself with his human needs and desires is included among these men. Nonetheless, suppose that I have ordered a Parisian frock coat from a tailor, and he brings me a Roman toga because it is more in accord with the eternal law of Beauty! *The first freedom of the press consists in its not being a business*. The writer who debases it to a material means deserves a punishment of his intrinsic lack of freedom, the extrinsic lack of freedom, censorship; better yet, his existence is already his punishment.

MARX, from: *Economic and Philosophic Manuscripts of 1844*

We have seen what significance, given socialism, the *wealth* of human needs has, and what significance, therefore, both a *new mode of production* and a new *object* of production have: a new manifestation of the forces of *human* nature and a new enrichment of *human* nature. Under private property their significance is reversed: every person speculates on creating a *new* need in another so as to drive him to a fresh sacrifice, to place him in a new dependence and to seduce him into a new mode of *gratification* and therefore economic ruin. Each person tries to establish over the other an *alien* power, so as thereby to find satisfaction of his own selfish need. The increase in the quantity of objects is accompanied by an extension of the realm of the alien powers to which man is subjected, and every new product represents a new *potency* of mutual swindling and mutual plundering. Man becomes ever poorer as man; his need for *money* becomes ever greater if he wants to overpower hostile being; and the power of his *money* declines exactly in inverse proportion to the increase in the volume of production: that is, his neediness grows as the *power* of money increases.

The need for money is therefore the true need produced by the modern economic system, and it is the only need which the latter produces. The *quantity* of money becomes to an ever greater degree its sole *effective* attribute: just as it reduces everything to its abstract form, so it reduces itself in the course of its own movement to something merely *quantitative*. *Excess* and *intemperance* come to be its true norm. Subjectively, this is even partly manifested in that the extension of products and needs falls into *contriving* and ever-*calculating* subservience to inhuman, refined, unnatural and *imaginary* appetites. Private property does not know how to change crude need into *human* need. Its *idealism* is *fantasy, caprice* and *whim*; and no eunuch flatters his despot more basely or uses more despicable means to stimulate his dulled capacity for pleasure in order to sneak a favor for himself than does the industrial eunuch—the producer —in order to sneak for himself a few pennies—in order to charm the golden birds out of the pockets of his Christianly beloved neighbors. He puts himself at the service of the other's most depraved fancies, plays the pimp between him and his need, excites in him morbid appetites, lies in wait for each of his weaknesses—all so that he can then demand the cash for this service of love. (Every product is a bait with which to seduce away the other's very being, his money; every real and possible need is a weakness which will lead the fly to the gluepot. General exploitation of communal human nature, just as every imperfection in man, is a bond with heaven—an avenue giving the priest access to his heart; every need is an opportunity to approach one's neighbor under the guise of the utmost amiability and to say to him: Dear friend, I give you what you need, but you know the *conditio sine qua non*; you know the ink in which you have to sign yourself over to me; in providing for your pleasure, I fleece you.)

And partly, this estrangement manifests itself in that it produces refinement of needs and of their means of satisfaction on the one hand, and a bestial barbarization, a complete, unrefined, abstract simplicity of need, on the other....

How the multiplication of needs and of their means of satisfaction breeds the absence of needs and of means is demonstrated by the political economist (and the capitalist: it should be noted that it is always *empirical* businessmen we are talking about when we refer to political economists—their *scientific* confession and mode of being)....

This science of marvelous industry is simultaneously the science of *asceticism*, and its true ideal is the *ascetic* but *extortionate* miser and the *ascetic* but *productive* slave. Its moral ideal is the *worker* who takes part of his wages to the savings-bank. And it has even found ready-made an abject *art* in which to clothe this its pet idea: they have presented it, bathed in sentimentality, on the stage. Thus political economy —despite its worldly and wanton appearance—is a true moral science, the most moral of all the sciences. Self-denial, the denial of life and of all human needs, is its cardinal doctrine. The less you eat, drink and read books; the less you go to the theatre, the dance hall, the public-house; the less you think, love, theorize, sing, paint, fence, etc., the more you *save*—the *greater* becomes your treasure which neither moths nor dust will devour—your *capital*. The less you *are*, the more you *have*; the less you express your own life, the greater is your *alienated* life—the greater is the store of your estranged being. Everything which the political economist takes from you in life and in humanity, he replaces for you in *money* and in *wealth*; and all the things which you cannot do, your money can do. It can eat and drink, go to the dance hall and the theatre; it can travel, it can appropriate art, learning, the treasures of the past, political power—all this it *can* appropriate for you—it can buy all this for you: it is the true *endowment*. Yet being all this, it is *inclined* to do nothing but create itself, buy itself; for everything else is after all its servant. And when I have the master I have the servant and do not need his servant. All passions and all activity must therefore be submerged in avarice. . . .

To be sure, the industrial capitalist also takes his pleasures. He does not by any means return to the unnatural simplicity of need; but his pleasure is only a side-issue—recuperation—something subordinated to production: at the same time it is a *calculated* and, therefore, itself an *economical* pleasure. For he debits it to his capital's expense-account, and what is squandered on his pleasure must therefore amount to no more than will be replaced with profit through the reproduction of capital.

MARX, from: *Pre-Capitalist Economic Formations* (1858)

The ancient conception, in which man always appears (in however narrowly national, religious or political a definition) as the aim of production, seems much more exalted than the modern conception, in which production is the aim of man and wealth the aim of production. In fact, however, when the narrow bourgeois form has been peeled away, what is wealth if not the universality of needs, capacities, enjoyments, productive powers, etc., of individuals, produced in universal exchange? What, if not the full development of human control over the forces of nature—those of his own nature as well as those of so-called "nature"? What, if not the absolute elaboration of his creative dispositions, without any preconditions other than antecedent historical evolution which makes the totality of this evolution—i.e., the evolution of all human powers as such, unmeasured by any *previously established* yardstick—an end in itself? What, if not a situation where man does not reproduce himself in any determined form, but produces his totality, where he does not seek to remain something formed by the past, but is in the absolute movement of becoming? In bourgeois political economy—and in the epoch of production to which it corresponds—this complete elaboration of what lies within man appears as the total alienation, and the destruction of all fixed, one-sided purposes as the sacrifice of the end in itself to a wholly external compulsion. Hence in one way the childlike world of the ancients appears to be superior; and this is so, in so far as we seek for closed shape, form and established limitation. The ancients provide a narrow satisfaction, whereas the modern world leaves us unsatisfied, or, where it appears to be satisfied with itself, is *vulgar* and *mean*.

MARX, from: *Theories of Surplus Value* (1861-62)

Because Storch* does not historically grasp material production itself—he sees it in general as the production of material goods, not as a definite, historically developed and specific form of this production—he loses the only footing that would allow him to grasp in part the ideological components of the ruling classes, in part the free** intellectual production of this given social formation. He cannot get beyond general and inept modes of expression. Thus, too, the relationship is not as simple as he assumes. For example, capitalist production is hostile to certain aspects of intellectual production, such as art and poetry. Looked at otherwise, the result would be like the conceit of the French in the eighteenth century, which Lessing so beautifully mocked. Since we have gone beyond the ancients in mechanics, etc., why shouldn't we also be able to bring forth an epic? In place of the *Iliad*, the *Henriad*!***

---

* H. Storch (1766-1835), Russian economist, author of a study of political economy; polemicized against Adam Smith.
** The word may also be read as *fein* (subtle), according to the editor of the original manuscript.
*** *Henriade*, an epic poem by Voltaire.

ENGELS, from: Introduction to *Dialectics of Nature* (1876)

In the manuscripts saved from the fall of Byzantium, in the antique statues dug out of the ruins of Rome, a new world was revealed to the astonished West, that of ancient Greece; the ghosts of the Middle Ages vanished before its shining forms; Italy rose to an undreamt-of flowering of art, which seemed like a reflection of classical antiquity and was never attained again. In Italy, France and Germany a new literature arose, the first modern literature; shortly afterwards came the classical epochs of English and Spanish literature....

It was the greatest progressive revolution that mankind had so far experienced, a time which called for giants and produced giants—giants in power of thought, passion and character, in universality and learning. The men who founded the modern rule of the bourgeoisie had anything but bourgeois limitations. On the contrary, the adventurous character of the time imbued them to a greater or less degree. There was hardly any man of importance then living who had not travelled extensively, who did not command four or five languages, who did not shine in a number of fields. Leonardo da Vinci was not only a great painter but also a great mathematician, mechanician and engineer, to whom the most diverse branches of physics are indebted for important discoveries; Albrecht Dürer was painter, engraver, sculptor, architect, and in addition invented a system of fortification embodying many of the ideas that much later were again taken up by Montalembert and the modern German science of fortification. Machiavelli was statesman, historian, poet, and at the same time the first notable military author of modern times. Luther not only cleansed the Augean stable of the Church but also that of the German language; he created modern German prose and composed the text and melody of that triumphal hymn which became the *Marseillaise* of the sixteenth century. For the heroes of that time had not yet come under the servitude of the division of labor, the restricting effects of which, with their production of one-sidedness, we so often notice in their successors. But what is especially characteristic of them is that they almost all pursue their lives and activities in the midst of the contemporary movements, in the practical struggle; they take sides and join in the fight, one by speaking and writing, another with the sword, many with both. Hence the fullness and force of character that makes them complete men.

COMMUNISM AND THE ADVENT
OF ARTISTIC DISALIENATION

MARX, from: *Economic and Philosophic Manuscripts of 1844*

It will be seen how in place of the *wealth* and *poverty* of
political economy come the *rich human being* and rich *human*
need. The *rich* human being is simultaneously the human
being *in need of* a totality of human life-activities—the man in
whom his own realization exists as an inner necessity, as *need.*
Not only *wealth*, but likewise the *poverty* of man—given
socialism—receives in equal measure a *human* and therefore
social significance. Poverty is the passive bond which causes
the human being to experience the need of the greatest
wealth—the *other* human being. The dominion of the objective
being in me, the sensuous outburst of my essential activity, is
emotion, which thus becomes here the *activity* of my being.

A *being* only considers himself independent when he stands
on his own feet; and he only stands on his own feet when he
owes his *existence* to himself. A man who lives by the grace of
another regards himself as a dependent being. But I live
completely by the grace of another if I owe him not only the
sustenance of my life, but if he has, moreover, *created* my
life—if he is the *source* of my life, and if it is not of my own
creation, my life has necessarily a source of this kind outside
it. The *Creation* is therefore an idea very difficult to dislodge
from popular consciousness. The self-mediated being of nature
and of man is *incomprehensible* to it, because it contradicts
everything *palpable* in practical life....

The transcendence of private property is therefore the
complete *emancipation* of all human senses and attributes; but
it is this emancipation precisely because these senses and
attributes have become, subjectively and objectively, *human.*
The eye has become a *human* eye, just as its *object* has
become a social, *human* object—an object emanating from
man for man. The *senses* have therefore become directly in
their practice *theoreticians.* They relate themselves to the *thing*
for the sake of the thing, but the thing itself is an *objective
human* relation to itself and to man,* and vice versa. Need or
enjoyment have consequently lost their *egotistical* nature, and
nature has lost its mere *utility* by use becoming *human* use....

This *material*, immediately *sensuous* private property, is the
material sensuous expression of *estranged human* life. Its
movement—production and consumption—is the *sensuous*
revelation of the movement of all production hitherto—i.e., the

* In practice I can relate myself to a thing humanly only if the thing
relates itself to the human being humanly. [Note by Marx.]

realization or the reality of man. Religion, family, state, law, morality, science, art, etc., are only *particular* modes of production, and fall under its general law. The positive transcendence of *private property* as the appropriation of *human* life is, therefore, the positive transcendence of all estrangement—that is to say, the return of man from religion, family, state, etc., to his *human*, i.e., *social* mode of existence. Religious estrangement as such occurs only in the realm of *consciousness*, of man's inner life, but economic estrangement is that of *real life*: its transcendence therefore embraces both aspects....

Communism is the *positive* transcendence of *private property*, as *human self-estrangement*, and therefore, is the real *appropriation of the human* essence by and for man; communism, therefore, is the complete return of man to himself as a *social* (i.e., human) being—a return become conscious, and accomplished within the entire wealth of previous development. This communism, as fully-developed naturalism, equals humanism, and as fully-developed humanism equals naturalism; it is the *genuine* resolution of the conflict between man and nature and between man and man— the true resolution of the strife between existence and essence, between objectification and self-confirmation, between freedom and necessity, between the individual and the species. Communism is the riddle of history solved, and it knows itself to be this solution....

When I am active *scientifically*, etc.,—when I am engaged in activity which I can seldom perform in direct community with others—then I am *social*, because I am active as a *man*. Not only is the material of my activity given to me as a social product (as is even the language in which the thinker is active): my *own* existence *is* social activity, and therefore, that which I make of myself, I make of myself for society and with the consciousness of myself as a social being.

My *general* consciousness is only the *theoretical* shape of that of which the *living* shape is the *real* community, the social fabric, although at the present day *general* consciousness is an abstraction from real life and as such antagonistically confronts it. Consequently, too, the *activity* of my general consciousness, as an activity, is my *theoretical* existence as a social being.

What is to be avoided above all is the re-establishing of "Society" as an abstraction *vis-à-vis* the individual. The individual is *the social being*. His life, even if it may not appear in the direct form of a *communal* life carried out together with others is, therefore, an expression and confirmation of *social life*. Man's individual and species life are not *different*, however much—and this is inevitable—the mode of existence of the individual is a more *particular*, or a more *general* mode of the life of the species, or the life of the species is a more *particular* or a more *general* individual life.

In his *consciousness of species* man confirms his real *social life* and simply repeats his real existence in thought, just as conversely the being of the species confirms itself in species-consciousness and is for *itself* in its generality as a thinking being.

Man, much as he may therefore be a *particular* individual (and it is precisely his particularity which makes him an individual, and a real *individual* social being), is just as much the *totality*—the ideal totality—the subjective existence of thought and experienced society present for itself; just as he exists also in the real world as the awareness and the real enjoyment of social existence, and as a totality of human life-activity.

Thinking and being are thus no doubt *distinct*, but at the same time they are in *unity* with each other.

MARX and ENGELS, from: *The German Ideology* (1845-46)

The exclusive concentration of artistic talent in particular individuals, and its suppression in the broad mass which is bound up with this, is a consequence of division of labor. If, even in certain social conditions, everyone was an excellent painter, that would not at all exclude the possibility of each of them being also an original painter, so that here too the difference between "human" and "unique" labor amounts to sheer nonsense. In any case, with a communist organization of society, there disappears the subordination of the artist to local and national narrowness, which arises entirely from division of labor, and also the subordination of the artist to some definite art, thanks to which he is exclusively a painter, sculptor, etc., the very name of his activity adequately expressing the narrowness of his professional development and his dependence on division of labor. In a communist society there are no painters but at most people who engage in painting among other activities.

MARX and ENGELS, from: *Manifesto of the Communist Party* (1848)

All objections urged against the Communistic mode of producing and appropriating material products have, in the same way, been urged against the Communistic modes of producing and appropriating intellectual products. Just as, to the bourgeois, the disappearance of class property is the disappearance of production itself, so the disappearance of class culture is to him identical with the disappearance of all culture.

That culture, the loss of which he laments, is, for the enormous majority, a mere training to act as a machine.

But don't wrangle with us so long as you apply to our intended abolition of bourgeois property the standard of your bourgeois notions of freedom, culture, law, etc. Your very ideas are but the outgrowth of the conditions of your bourgeois production and bourgeois property....

Does it require deep intuition to comprehend that man's ideas, views and conceptions, in one word, man's consciousness, change with every change in the conditions of his material existence, in his social relations and his social life?

What else does the history of ideas prove than that intellectual production changes its character in proportion as material production is changed? The ruling ideas of each age have ever been the ideas of its ruling class....

In place of the old bourgeois society, with its classes and class antagonisms, we shall have an association in which the free development of each is the condition for the free development of all.

ENGELS, from: *The Housing Question* (1872)

For Proudhon*...the whole industrial revolution of the last hundred years, the introduction of steam power and large-scale factory production which substitutes machinery for hand labor and increases the productivity of labor a thousandfold, is a highly repugnant occurrence, something which really ought never to have taken place. The petty-bourgeois Proudhon

* Pierre Joseph Proudhon (1809-1865), French socialist whose ideas were taken over by the anarchist movement.

aspires to a world in which each person turns out a separate and independent product that is immediately consumable and exchangeable in the market. Then, as long as each person receives back the full value of his labor in the form of another product,"eternal justice" is satisfied and the best possible world created. But this best possible world of Proudhon has already been nipped in the bud and trodden underfoot by the advance of industrial development, which long ago destroyed individual labor in all the big branches of industry and which is destroying it daily more and more in the smaller and even smallest branches, which is setting social labor supported by machinery and the harnessed forces of nature in its place, and whose finished product, immediately exchangeable or consumable, is the joint work of the many individuals through whose hands it has had to pass. And it is precisely this industrial revolution which has raised the productive power of human labor to such a high level that—for the first time in the history of mankind—the possibility exists, given a rational division of labor among all, of producing not only enough for the plentiful consumption of all members of society and for an abundant reserve fund, but also of leaving each individual sufficient leisure so that what is really worth preserving in historically inherited culture—science, art, forms of intercourse—may not only be preserved but converted from a monopoly of the ruling class into the common property of the whole of society, and may be further developed. And here is the decisive point: as soon as the productive power of human labor has risen to this height, every excuse disappears for the existence of a ruling class. After all, the ultimate basis on which class differences were defended was always: there must be a class which need not plague itself with the production of its daily subsistence, in order that it may have time to look after the intellectual work of society. This talk, which up to now had its great historical justification, has been cut off at the root once and for all by the industrial revolution of the last hundred years. The existence of a ruling class is becoming daily more and more a hindrance to the development of industrial productive power, and equally so to that of science, art and especially forms of cultural intercourse. There never were greater boors than our modern bourgeois.

CLASS VALUES IN LITERATURE

MARX, from: *The Holy Family* (1845)

The opposition between "good" and "evil" confronts the Critical Hercules* when he is still a youth in two personifications, *Murph* and *Polidori*, both of them Rudolph's teachers. The former educates him in good and is "*good*." The latter educates him in evil and is "*evil*." In order that this conception should by no means be inferior in triviality to similar conceptions in other novels, Murph, the personification of "*good*" cannot be "learned" or "particularly endowed intellectually." But he is *honest, simple*, and *laconic;* he feels himself great when he applies to evil such clipped words as "*foul*" or "*vile*," and has *horreur* for anything which is *base*. To use Hegel's expression, he sets the good and the true in equality of tones, i.e., in *one note*.

Polidori, on the contrary, is a prodigy of cleverness, knowledge, and education, and at the same time of the "most dangerous immorality," having, in particular, what Eugène Sue, as a member of the young devout French bourgeoisie, could not forget—"*the most frightful scepticism*." We can judge of the moral energy and education of Eugène Sue and his hero by their panicky fear of *scepticism*.

"Murph," says Herr Szeliga, "is at the same time the perpetuated guilt of January 13 and the perpetual redemption of that guilt by his incomparable love and self-sacrifice for the person of Rudolph."

As Rudolph is the *deus ex machina* and the mediator of the world, Murph in turn is Rudolph's personal *deus ex machina* and mediator.

"Rudolph and the salvation of mankind, Rudolph and the realization of the essential perfections of mankind are for Murph an inseparable unity, a unity to which he dedicates himself not with the stupid canine devotion of the slave, but knowingly and independently."

So Murph is an enlightened, knowing and independent slave. Like every prince's valet, he sees in his master the

* A sarcastic nickname which Marx applies to a central character, Rudolph, in Eugène Sue's *Les Mystères de Paris*. This novel is extensively discussed by Marx and Engels in *The Holy Family or Critique of Critical Criticism*, partly for its own class-conditioned limitations as social fiction, and partly as a basis to further criticize one of its approving critics, Zychlinski, called Szeliga, who belonged to a Young Hegelian group of left intellectuals with whom Marx had earlier broken, owing to their moralistic preference of intellectual-elitist qualities, more or less typified in turn by the character Rudolph.

salvation of mankind personified. *Graun* flatters Murph with the words: *"fearless bodyguard."* Rudolph himself calls him a *model servant*, and truly he is a *model servant*. Eugène Sue tells us that Murph scrupulously addresses Rudolph as "Monseigneur" when alone with him. In the presence of others he calls him "Monsieur" with his lips to keep his incognity, but "Monseigneur" with his heart.

"Murph helps to raise the veil from the mysteries, but only for Rudolph's sake. He helps to destroy the power of mystery."

The denseness of the veil with which Murph envelopes the simplest things of this world can be seen by his conversation with the envoy Graun. From the legal right of self-defense in case of emergency he concludes that Rudolph, as *judge of the secret court*, was entitled to blind the gang leader, although the latter was in chains and "defenseless." His description of how Rudolph will tell of his "noble" actions before the assizes, what eloquence and fine phrases he will display, and how he will let his great heart pour forth could have been written by a *Gymnasiast* [high school student] just after reading Schiller's *Robbers*. . . .

The gang leader is a criminal of herculean strength and great moral energy. He was brought up an educated and well-schooled man. This passionate athlete clashes with the laws and customs of bourgeois society whose universal yardstick is mediocrity, delicate morals and quiet trade. He becomes a murderer and abandons himself to all the excesses of a violent temperament that can nowhere find a fitting human occupation.

Rudolph captures this criminal. He wants to reform him critically and set him as an example for the *world of law*. He quarrels with the world of law not over *"punishment"* itself, but over *kinds* and *methods* of punishment. . . . Rudolph has not the slightest idea that one can rise *above* criminal experts: his ambition is to be *"the greatest criminal expert," primus inter pares*. He has the gang leader *blinded* by the Negro doctor David. . . .

The gang leader has abused his strength; Rudolph paralyzes, lames, destroys that strength. There is no more *Critical* means of getting rid of the incorrect manifestations of the essential force of man than to annihilate that essential force. This is the Christian means—plucking out the eye or cutting off the hand if it scandalizes; in a word, killing the body if the body scandalizes; for the eye, the hand, the body are really but superfluous sinful appendages of man. Human nature must be killed in order to heal its illnesses. . . .

Eugène Sue satisfies his monkish, bestial lust in the *self-humiliation* of man to the extent of making the gang leader implore the old hag *Chouette* and the little imp *Tortillard* on his knees not to abandon him. . . .

The idea of the punishment that Rudolph carried out in blinding the gang leader—the isolation of the man and his soul from the outer world, the association of legal penalty with theological torture—is decisively implemented in the *cell system*. That is why Monsieur Sue glorifies that system. . . .

Eugène Sue's personages—earlier *Chourineur* and now the gang leader—must express, as the result of their *own* thoughts, the conscious motive of their acts, the reason why the writer makes them behave in a certain way and no other. They must continually say: I have amended in this, in that, etc. As they do not really come to a life of any content, what they say must give vigorous tones to insignificant features like the protection of *Fleur de Marie*.

MARX and ENGELS, from: *The German Ideology* (1845-46)

It depends not on *consciousness*, but on *being*; not on thought but on life; it depends on the empirical development and manifestation of life of the individual, which in turn depends on conditions in the world. If the circumstances in which the individual lives allow him only the [one]-sided development of a single quality at the expense of all the rest, if they give him the material and time to develop only that one quality, then this individual achieves only a one-sided, crippled development. No moral preaching avails here. . . . In the case of an individual, for example, whose life embraces a wide circle of varied activities and practical relations to the world, and who, therefore, lives a many-sided life, thought has the same character of universality as every other manifestation of his life. . . . The fact that under favorable circumstances some individuals are able to rid themselves of their local narrow-mindedness is not at all because the individuals by their reflection imagine that they have gotten rid of, or intended to get rid of, this local narrow-mindedness, but because they, in their empirical reality, and owing to empirical needs, have been able to bring about world intercourse.

ENGELS, from: "German Socialism in Verse and Prose, II," (1847)

Goethe stands in his works in a double relation to the German society of his time. Sometimes he is hostile to it: he tries to escape its odiousness, as in the *Iphigenia* and in general during the Italian journey; he rebels against it as Goetz, Prometheus, and Faust; he scorches it with his bitterest scorn as Mephistopheles. On the other hand, he is sometimes friendly to it, "accomodates" himself to it as in most of the *Tame Epigrams* and in many prose writings, celebrates it as in the *Masquerades*, even defends it against the intruding historical movement, particularly in all the writings where he happens to speak of the French Revolution. Goethe does not simply acknowledge particular sides of German life in opposition to others that are repugnant to him. Generally it depends on the various moods in which he finds himself; there is a continual struggle in himself between the poet of genius, who is disgusted by the wretchedness of his surroundings, and the Frankfurt alderman's cautious child, the privy councilor of Weimar, who sees himself obliged to make truce with it and to get used to it. Thus Goethe is sometimes colossal, sometimes petty; other times a defiant, ironical, world-scorning genius, or a considerate, complacent, narrow philistine. Even Goethe was unable to overcome the wretchedness of German life (*die deutsche Misère*); on the contrary, it overcame him, and this victory over the greatest German is the best proof that the wretchedness cannot be conquered by the individual "through intellectual means." Goethe was too universal, too active a nature, too physical to seek escape from this wretchedness in a flight as Schiller did in the Kantian ideal: he was too sharp-sighted not to see how this flight finally came down to an exchange of a commonplace for a highflown wretchedness. His temperament, his energies, his whole intellectual tendency directed him towards practical life, and the practical life that he encountered was miserable. This dilemma—to exist in a sphere of life that he had to despise, and at the same time, to be fettered to this sphere as the only one in which he could fulfill himself—was the one in which Goethe continually found himself, and, the older he became, the more retiring did the powerful poet become, *de guerre lasse* [weary of war], hiding behind the insignificant Weimar minister. We are not criticizing Goethe, *a la* Börne and Menzel,* for not being a

* Ludwig Börne (1786-1837), a spokesman of the 'Young Germany' movement admired by a younger Engels who had wanted to pursue a

liberal, but for being a philistine at times; we do not assert that he was incapable of any enthusiasm for German freedom, but that he sacrificed his sounder aesthetic feeling, which did occasionally break through, to a small-town aversion of every great contemporary historical movement. We do not accuse him of being a courtier, but of managing with a ceremonial serious-ness the most trivial affairs and the *menus plaisirs* [minute details] of one of the most trivial little German courts at a time when a Napoleon was cleaning out the vast Augean stables of Germany. In general, we are reproaching him neither from moral nor from partisan standpoints, but chiefly from aesthetic and historical standpoints; we are measuring Goethe neither by a moral, nor by a political, nor by a "humane" standpoint.

ENGELS, from: "The Manifesto of M. de Lamartine" (1847)

You recently published this curious piece of workmanship. It consists of two very distinct parts: *political* measures and *social* measures. Now all the political measures are taken from the constitution of 1791, with almost no alteration; that means, they are a return to the demands of the bourgeoisie in the beginning of the revolution. At that time the entire bourgeoisie, including even the smaller tradesmen, were invested with political power, while at present only the big capitalists share in this power. What, then, is the meaning of the political measures proposed by M. de Lamartine?* To place the government into the hands of the petty bourgeoisie, but under the semblance of giving it to the whole people (this, and nothing else, is the meaning of his universal suffrage, with his double system of elections). And his *social* measures? Why they are either things which presuppose that a successful revolution has already given political power to the people—such as free education for all; or measures of pure charity, that is, measures to keep down the revolutionary

_____

literary career in its image; and Wolfgang Menzel (1798-1873), major critic of the day, who attacked the 'Young Germany' movement, and Goethe as well.

   * Alphonse de Lamartine (1790-1869), French Romantic poet, historian, and bourgeois politician, became the head of the provisional Republican government of February 1848. Engels's letter is to *The Northern Star*, the English Chartist newspaper, which had printed extracts from Lamartine's manifesto on French political problems. The next three selections also center on Lamartine.

energies of the proletarians; or mere high-sounding words without any practical meaning, such as extinction of mendicity by order of the council, abolition of public poverty by law, a ministry for the welfare of the people, etc. They are, therefore, either totally useless to the people, or calculated to guarantee them just many advantages that will assure some sort of public tranquility, or they are mere empty promises, which no man can keep—and in these two last cases they are worse than useless. In short, M. de Lamartine proves himself, both from a social and a political point of view, the faithful representative of the small tradesman, the petty bourgeoisie, and he shares the same illusion of this class: that he represents the working people.

MARX, from: "The Revolutionary Movement" (1849)*

Never was a revolutionary movement begun with such a spiritually uplifting overture as the revolutionary movement of 1848. The Pope offered the Church's blessing; Lamartine's Aeolian harp trembled to gentle-sounding philanthropical melodies whose text was *fraternite*, the fraternization of society's parts and the nations.

> *Seid umschlungen Millionen,*
> *diesen Kuss der Ganzen Welt!***

* This article on "The Revolutionary Movement" appeared in the *Neue Rheinische Zeitung*, edited by Marx; it was the chief organ of the proletarian wing in the fight for German democracy.
** From Schiller, "Hymn to Joy." Used by Beethoven in the last movement of his Ninth Symphony:

> *Millions, be you embraced!*
> *For the Universe, this kiss!*

MARX, from: *The Class Struggles in France 1848-1850* (1850)

Lamartine in the Provisional Government, this was at first no real interest, no definite class; this was the February Revolution itself, the common uprising with its illusions, its poetry, its visionary content and its phrases. For the rest, the spokesman of the February Revolution, by his position and his views, belonged to the *bourgeoisie*.

If Paris, as a result of political centralization, rules France, then the workers, in moments of revolutionary earthquakes, rule Paris. The first act in the life of the Provisional Government was an attempt to escape from this overpowering influence by an appeal from intoxicated Paris to sober France. Lamartine disputed the right of the barricade fighters to proclaim a republic on the ground that only the majority of Frenchmen had that right; they must await their votes; the Paris proletariat must not besmirch its victory by a usurpation. The bourgeoisie allows the proletariat only one usurpation—that of fighting. . . .

At that time all the royalists were transformed into republicans and all the millionaires of Paris into workers. The phrase which corresponded to this imaginary abolition of class relations was *fraternité,* universal fraternization and brotherhood. This pleasant abstraction from class antagonisms, this sentimental reconciliation of contradictory class interests, this visionary elevation above the class struggle, this *fraternité* was the real catchword of the February Revolution. The classes were divided by a mere *misunderstanding* and Lamartine baptized the Provisional Government on February 24 "un gouvernement qui suspende *ce malentendu terrible qui existe entre les différentes classes.*" The Paris proletariat revelled in this magnanimous intoxication of fraternity. . . .

The official representatives of French democracy were steeped in republican ideology to such an extent that it was only some weeks later that they began to have an inkling of the significance of the June fight. They were stupefied by the gunpowder smoke in which their fantastic republic dissolved. The reader will allow us to describe our immediate impression of the June defeat in the words of the *Neue Rheinische Zeitung*:

"The last official remnant of the February Revolution, the Executive Commission, has melted away, like an apparition, before the seriousness of events. The fireworks of Lamartine have turned into the war rockets of Cavaignac. *Fraternité,* the fraternity of antagonistic classes, of which one exploits the other, this *fraternité,* proclaimed in February, written in capital letters on the brow of Paris, on every prison, on every barracks—its true, unadulterated, prosaic expression is *civil war,* civil war in its most frightful form, the war of labor and capital. This fraternity flamed in front of all the windows of Paris on the evening of June 25, when the Paris of the bourgeoisie was illuminated, while the Paris of the proletariat burnt, bled, moaned unto death. Fraternity endured just as long as the interests of the bourgeoisie were in fraternity with the interests of the proletariat.

"Pedants of the old revolutionary traditions of 1793; socialist systematizers who begged at the doors of the bourgeoisie on behalf of the people and were allowed to preach long sermons and to compromise themselves as long as the proletarian lion had to be lulled to sleep; republicans who demanded the old bourgeois order in its entirety, with the exception of the crowned head; adherents of the dynasty among the opposition upon whom accident foisted the overthrow of the dynasty instead of a change of ministers; Legitimists who did not want to cast aside the livery but to change its cut—these were the allies with whom the people made its February.—The February Revolution was the *beautiful* revolution, the revolution of universal sympathy, because the antagonisms which had flared up in it against the monarchy slumbered *undeveloped*, harmoniously side by side, because the social struggle which formed its background had won only an airy existence, an existence of phrases, of words. The *June Revolution* is the *ugly* revolution, the repulsive revolution, because deeds have taken the place of phrases....

MARX, from: *The Eighteenth Brumaire of Louis Bonaparte* (1852)

Thus arose the Social-Democracy. The new *Montagne*, the result of this combination, contained, apart from some supernumeraries from the working class and some socialist sectarians, the same elements as the old *Montagne*, only numerically stronger. However, in the course of development, it had changed with the class that it represented. The peculiar character of the Social-Democracy is epitomized in the fact that democratic-republican institutions are demanded as a means, not of doing away with two extremes, capital and wage labor, but of weakening their antagonism and transforming it into harmony. However different the means proposed for the attainment of this end may be, however much it may be trimmed with more or less revolutionary notions, the content remains the same. This content is the transformation of society in a democratic way, but a transformation within the bounds of the petty bourgeoisie. Only one must not form the narrow-minded notion that the petty bourgeoisie, on principle, wishes to enforce an egoistic class interest. Rather, it believes that the *special* conditions of its emancipation are the *general* conditions within the frame of which alone modern society can be saved and the class struggle avoided. Just as little must one imagine that the democratic representatives are indeed all shopkeepers or enthusiastic champions of shopkeepers. According to their education and their individual position they may be as far apart as heaven from earth. What makes them representatives of the petty bourgeoisie is the fact that in their minds they do not get beyond the limits which the latter do not get beyond in life, that they are consequently driven, theoretically, to the same problems and solutions to which material interest and social position drive the latter practically. This is, in general, the relationship between the *political* and *literary representatives* of a class and the class they represent.

MARX, from: Preface to *A Contribution to the Critique of Political Economy* (1859)

In the social production of their life, men enter into definite relations that are indispensable and independent of their will, relations of production which correspond to a definite state of the development of their material productive forces. The sum total of these relations of production constitutes the economic structure of society, the real foundation, on which rises a legal and political superstructure and to which correspond definite forms of social consciousness. The mode of production of material life conditions the social, political and intellectual life process in general. It is not the consciousness of men that determines their being, but, on the contrary, their social being that determines their consciousness. At a certain stage of their development, the material productive forces of society come in conflict with the existing relations of production, or—what is but a legal expression for the same thing—with the property relations within which they have been at work hitherto. From forms of development of the productive forces these relations turn into their fetters. Then begins an epoch of social revolution. With the change of the economic foundation the entire immense superstructure is more or less rapidly transformed. In considering such transformations a distinction should always be made between the material transformation of the economic conditions of production, which can be determined with the precision of natural science, and the legal, political, religious, aesthetic or philosophic—in short, ideological forms in which men become conscious of this conflict and fight it out. Just as our opinion of an individual is not based on what he thinks of himself, so can we not judge of such a period of transformation by its own consciousness; on the contrary, this consciousness must be explained rather from the contradictions of material life, from the existing conflict between the social productive forces and the relations of production.

ENGELS, from: *Ludwig Feuerbach and the End of Classical German Philosophy* (1886)

Just as in France in the eighteenth century, so in Germany in the nineteenth, a philosophical revolution ushered in the political collapse. But how different the two looked! The French were in open combat against all official science, against the church and often also against the state; their writings were printed across the frontier, in Holland or England, while they themselves were often in jeopardy of imprisonment in the Bastille. On the other hand, the Germans were professors, state-appointed instructors of youth; their writings were recognized textbooks, and the terminating system of the whole development—the Hegelian system—was even raised, as it were, to the rank of a royal Prussian philosophy of state! Was it possible that a revolution could hide behind these professors, behind their obscure, pedantic phrases, their ponderous, wearisome sentences? Were not precisely those people who were then regarded as the representatives of the revolution, the liberals, the bitterest opponents of this brain-confusing philosophy? But what neither the government nor the liberals saw was seen at least by one man as early as 1833, and this man was none other than Heinrich Heine.

ENGELS, from: Letter to Paul Ernst, June 5, 1890

Unfortunately I cannot comply with your request to write you a letter that you could use against Herr Bahr.* This would

* Hermann Bahr (1863-1934), the Austrian drama critic. Paul Ernst (1866-1933) was an editor of the German Social-Democrat Party journal of theory, *Die Neue Zeit*, in which he regularly wrote on literature and drama. He had recently debated the Scandinavian women's movement and its literary treatment with a writer from the *Freie Bühne für modernes Leben*, a magazine of German naturalism, on which Bahr was an editor. Ernst held that women's liberation could only result with the general, inevitable development of productive relations; he ridiculed as 'petty bourgeois' Ibsen and others who saw a moral and psychological issue. Bahr then jumped into the fray by attacking Ernst in a pair of articles, "The Epigones of Marxism," which defended what Bahr saw as

involve me in an open polemic against him, and for that I would literally have to rob myself of the time. What I write here, therefore, is intended only for you personally.

Furthermore, I am not at all acquainted with what you call the feminist movement in Scandinavia; I only know some of Ibsen's dramas and have not the slightest idea whether or to what extent Ibsen can be considered responsible for the more or less hysterical effusions of bourgeois and petty bourgeois women careerists.

On the other hand, the field covered by what is generally designated as the woman question is so vast that one cannot, within the confines of a letter, treat this subject thoroughly or say anything half-way satisfactory about it. This much is certain, that Marx could never have "adopted the attitude" ascribed to him by Herr Bahr; after all, he was not crazy.

As for your attempt to explain this matter from the materialist viewpoint, I must tell you from the very first that the materialist method is converted into its direct opposite if, instead of being used as a guiding thread in historical research, it is made to serve as a ready-cut pattern on which to tailor historical facts. And if Herr Bahr thinks he has caught you in a mistake, it seems to me that he is somewhat justified.

You classify all Norway, and everything happening there, as petty bourgeois, and then, without the slightest hesitation, you apply to this Norwegian petty bourgeoisie your ideas about the German petty bourgeoisie.

Now two facts stand in the way here.

In the first place: at a time when throughout all Europe the victory over Napoleon spelled a victory of reaction over revolution, when only in its homeland, France, was the revolution still capable of inspiring enough fear to wrest from the re-established Bourbons a bourgeois liberal constitution, Norway was able to secure a constitution far more democratic than any constitution in Europe at that time.

In the second place, during the course of the last twenty years Norway has had a literary renaissance unlike that of any other country of this period, except Russia. Petty bourgeois or not, these people are creating more than anywhere else, and stamping their imprint upon literature of other countries, including Germany.

---

the authentic Marxian view; and Ernst then requested this assistance from Engels. By 1890, Ernst was involved with the 'youth' faction of the party, about which Engels writes in the last document of this section. In 1891 Ernst was expelled from the Social-Democratic Party.

These facts demand, in my opinion, that we analyze the specific characteristics of the Norwegian petty bourgeoisie.

You will no doubt then perceive that we are here faced with a very important difference. In Germany the petty bourgeoisie is the product of an abortive revolution, of an arrested, thwarted development; it owes its peculiar and very marked characteristics of cowardice, narrowness, impotence and ineffectuality to the Thirty Years War and the ensuing period during which almost all of the other great nations were, on the contrary, developing rapidly. These traits remained with the German petty bourgeoisie even after Germany had again been carried into the stream of historical development; they were pronounced enough to engrave themselves upon all the other German social classes as more or less typically German, until the day when our working class broke through these narrow boundaries. The German workers are with justification all the more violently "without a country" in that they are entirely free of German petty bourgeois narrowness. Thus the German petty bourgeoisie does not constitute a normal historical phase, but an extremely exaggerated caricature, a phenomenon of degeneration. The petty bourgeoisie of England, France, etc., are on an altogether different level than the German petty bourgeoisie.

In Norway, on the other hand, the small peasantry and the petty bourgeoisie, together with a limited section of the middle class—just as in England and France in the seventeenth century, for example—have for several centuries represented the normal state of society. Here there can be no question of a violent return to outdated conditions as a consequence of some great defeated movement or a Thirty Years War. The country has lagged behind the times because of its isolation and natural conditions, but its situation has always corresponded to its conditions of production, and, therefore, been normal. Only very recently have manifestations of large scale industry sporadically made their appearance in the country, but that mighty lever of the concentration of capital, the Bourse, is lacking. Furthermore the powerful shipping industry also exerts a conservative influence, for while throughout the rest of the world steamboats are superseding sailing vessels, Norway is expanding her sailing vessel navigation considerably, and possesses if not the greatest then at all events the second greatest fleet of sailing ships in the world, belonging mostly to small shipowners, just as in England around 1720. Nevertheless, this circumstance has infused new vitality into the old lethargic existence, and this vitality has made itself felt also in the literary revival.

The Norwegian peasant has never known serfdom, and this fact gives an altogether different background to the whole development of the country, as it did in Castile. The Norwegian petty bourgeois is the son of a free peasant, and for this reason he is a *man* compared to the miserable German philistine. Likewise the Norwegian petty bourgeois woman is infinitely superior to the wife of a German philistine. And whatever the weaknesses of Ibsen's dramas, for instance, they undoubtedly reflect the world of the petty and the middle bourgeoisie, but a world totally different from the German world, a world where men are still possessed of character and initiative and the capacity for independent action, even though their behavior may seem odd to a foreign observer.

ENGELS, from: Letter to Paul Lafargue, August 27, 1890

There has been a students' revolt in the German Party. For the past 2-3 years, a crowd of students, literary men and other young declassed bourgeois has rushed into the Party, arriving just in time to occupy most of the editorial positions on the new journals which are sprouting and, as usual, they regard the bourgeois universities as a Socialist Staff College which gives them the right to enter the ranks of the party with an officer's if not a general's brevet. All these gentlemen go in for Marxism, but of the kind you were familiar with in France ten years ago and of which Marx said: "All I know is that I'm no Marxist!" And of these gentlemen he would probably have said what Heine said of his imitators: I sowed dragons and reaped fleas.

These worthy fellows, whose impotence is only matched by their arrogance, have found some support in the new recruits to the Party in Berlin—typical Berlinism, which is to be interpreted as presumption, cowardice, empty bluster and gift of the gab all rolled into one, seems to have come to the surface again for a moment; it provided the chorus for the student gentry.

ENGELS, from: Letter to Conrad Schmidt, October 27, 1890

As to the realms of ideology which soar still higher in the air,—religion, philosophy, etc.—these have a prehistoric stock, found already in existence by and taken over in the historic period of what we should today call bunk. These various false conceptions of nature, of man's own being, of spirits, magic forces, etc., have for the most part only a negative economic basis; the low economic development of the prehistoric period is supplemented and also partially conditioned and even caused by the false conceptions of nature. And even though economic necessity was the main driving force of the progressive knowledge of nature and becomes ever more so, it would surely be pedantic to try and find economic causes for all this primitive nonsense. The history of science is the history of the gradual clearing away of this nonsense or of its replacement by fresh but always less absurd nonsense. The people who attend to this belong in their turn to special spheres in the division of labor and appear to themselves to be working in an independent field. And to the extent that they form an independent group within the social division of labor, their productions, including their errors, react back as an influence upon the whole development of society, even on its economic development. But all the same they themselves are again under the dominating influence of economic development. In philosophy, for instance, this can be most readily proved for the bourgeois period. Hobbes was the first modern materialist (in the eighteenth-century sense) but he was an absolutist in a period when absolute monarchy was at its height throughout the whole of Europe and when the fight of absolute monarchy versus the people was beginning in England. Locke, both in religion and politics, was the child of the class compromise of 1688. The English deists and their more consistent continuators, the French materialists, were the true philosophers of the bourgeoisie, the French even of the bourgeois revolution. The German Philistine runs through German philosophy from Kant to Hegel, sometimes positively and sometimes negatively. But the philosophy of every epoch, since it is a definite sphere in the division of labor, has as its presupposition certain definite thought material handed down to it by its predecessors, from which it takes its start. And that is why economically backward countries can still play first fiddle in philosophy: France in the eighteenth century compared with England, on whose philosophy the French based themselves, and later Germany relatively to both. But in France as well as in Germany, philosophy and the general blossoming of literature at that time were the result of a rising economic development. I consider the ultimate supremacy of economic development established in these spheres too, but it comes to pass within the conditions imposed by the particular sphere itself: in philosophy, for instance, through the operation of economic influences (which again generally act only under political, etc., disguises) upon the existing philosophic material handed down by predecessors. Here economy creates nothing anew, but it determines the way in which the thought material found in existence is altered and further developed, and that too for the most part indirectly, for it is the political, legal and moral reflexes which exercise the greatest direct influence upon philosophy.

ENGELS, from: "Preface" to the Fourth Edition, *The Origin of the Family, Private Property and the State* (June 16, 1891)

Bachofen* points to the *Oresteia* of Aeschylus as a dramatic depiction of the struggle between the declining mother right and the rising, victorious father right in the Heroic Age. Clytemnestra has slain her husband Agamemnon, who has just returned from the Trojan War, for the sake of her lover Aegisthus; but Orestes, her son by Agamemnon, avenges his father's murder by slaying his mother. For this he is pursued by the Erinyes, the demonic defenders of mother right, according to which matricide is the most heinous and inexpiable of crimes. But Apollo, who through his oracle has incited Orestes to commit this deed, and Athena, who is called in as arbiter—the two deities which here represent the new order, based on father right—protect him. Athena hears both sides. The whole controversy is briefly summarized in the debate which now ensues between Orestes and the Erinyes. Orestes declares that Clytemnestra is guilty of a double outrage; for in killing *her* husband, she also killed *his* father. Why then have the Erinyes persecuted him and not Clytemnestra, who is much the greater culprit? The reply is striking:

"Unrelated by blood was she to the man that she slew." The murder of a man not related by blood, even though he be the husband of the murderess, is expiable and does not concern the Erinyes. Their function is to avenge only murders among blood-relatives, and the most heinous of all these, according to mother right, is matricide. Apollo now intervenes in defense of Orestes. Athena calls upon the Areopagites—the Athenian jurors—to vote on the question. The votes for acquittal and for the conviction are equal. Then Athena, as President of the Court, casts her vote in favor of Orestes and acquits him. Father right has gained the day over mother right. The "gods of junior lineage," as they are described by the Erinyes themselves,

---

* Johann Jakob Bachofen (1815-1887), Swiss historian, sociologist and jurist, the author of *Mother Right* (1861).

are victorious over the Erinyes, and the latter allow themselves finally to be persuaded to assume a new office in the service of the new order.

This new but absolutely correct interpretation of the *Oresteia* is one of the best and most beautiful passages in the whole book, but it shows at the same time that Bachofen himself believes in the Erinyes, Apollo, and Athena at least as much as Aeschylus did in his day; in fact, he believes that in the Heroic Age of Greece they performed the miracle of overthrowing mother right and replacing it by father right. Clearly, such a conception—which regards religion as the decisive lever in world history—must finally end in sheer mysticism. Therefore, it is an arduous and by no means always profitable task to wade through Bachofen's bulky quarto volume. But all this does not detract from his merit as a pioneer, for he was the first to substitute for mere phrases about an unknown primitive condition of promiscuous sexual intercourse concrete proof that ancient classical literature teems with traces of a condition that had in fact existed before monogamy among the Greeks and the Asiatics, in which not only a man had sexual intercourse with more than one woman, but a woman had sexual intercourse with more than one man, without violating the established custom; that this custom did not disappear without leaving traces in the form of the limited surrender by which women were compelled to purchase their right to monogamous marriage; that descent, therefore, could originally be reckoned only in the female line, from mother to mother; that this exclusive validity of the female line persisted far into the time of monogamy with assured, or at least recognized, paternity; and that this original position of the mother as the sole certain parent of her children assured her, and thus women in general, a higher social status than they have ever enjoyed since. Bachofen did not express these propositions as clearly as this—his mystical outlook prevented him from doing so; but he proved that they were correct, and this, in 1861, meant a complete revolution.

ENGELS, from: "Preface" to the Italian edition of *The Communist Manifesto* (February 1, 1892)

The close of the feudal Middle Ages and the onset of the modern capitalistic era are marked by a figure of grandiose stature: it is an Italian, Dante, who is both the last poet of the Middle Ages and the first modern poet. Today, just as it was around 1300, a new historical era is in the making. Will Italy provide us with a new Dante who will announce the birth of this new proletarian era?

THE CLASS RECEPTION OF ARTISTIC VALUES

MARX, from: *The Eighteenth Brumaire of Louis Bonaparte* (1852)

Hegel remarks somewhere that all facts and personages of great importance in world history occur, as it were, twice. He forgot to add: the first time as tragedy, the second as farce....

Men make their own history, but they do not make it just as they please; they do not make it under circumstances chosen by themselves, but under circumstances directly encountered, given and transmitted from the past. The tradition of all the dead generations weighs like a nightmare on the brain of the living. And just when they seem engaged in revolutionizing themselves and things, in creating something that has never yet existed, precisely in such periods of revolutionary crisis they anxiously conjure up the spirits of the past to their service and borrow from them names, battle cries and costumes in order to present the new scene of world history in this time-honored disguise and this borrowed language. Thus Luther donned the mask of the Apostle Paul, the Revolution of 1789 to 1814 draped itself alternately as the Roman Republic and the Roman empire, and the Revolution of 1848 knew nothing better to do than to parody, now 1789, now the revolutionary tradition of 1793 to 1795. In like manner a beginner who has learnt a new language always translates it back into his mother tongue, but he has assimilated the spirit of the new language and can freely express himself in it only when he finds his way in it without recalling the old and forgets his native tongue in the use of the new....

But unheroic as bourgeois society is, it nevertheless took heroism, sacrifice, terror, civil war and battles of peoples to bring it into being. And in the classically austere traditions of the Roman republic its gladiators found the ideals and the art forms, the self-deceptions that they needed in order to conceal from themselves the bourgeois limitations of the content of their struggles and to keep their enthusiasm on the high plane of the great historical tragedy. Similarly, at another stage of development, a century earlier, Cromwell and the English people had borrowed speech, passions and illusions from the Old Testament for their bourgeois revolution. When the real aim had been achieved, when the bourgeois transformation of English society had been accomplished, Locke supplanted Habakkuk.

Thus the awakening of the dead in those revolutions served the purpose of glorifying the new struggles, not of parodying the old; of magnifying the given task in imagination, not of fleeing from its solution in reality; of finding once more the spirit of revolution, not of making its ghost walk about again....

The social revolution of the nineteenth century cannot draw its poetry from the past, but only from the future. It cannot begin with itself before it has stripped off all superstition in regard to the past. Earlier revolutions required recollections of past world history in order to drug themselves concerning their own content. In order to arrive at its own content, the revolution of the nineteenth century must let the dead bury their dead. There the phrase went beyond the content; here the content goes beyond the phrase.

MARX, from: Letter to Ferdinand Lassalle, July 22, 1861

You have demonstrated that originally (and even today, if we consider the scientific insight of the juridical experts) the adoption of the Roman Testament [as a modern rule for inheritance law] rests on a misunderstanding. But it in no way follows that in its *modern* form the Testament—through whatever misunderstandings of Roman law the contemporary juridical experts may be able to reconstrue it—is the *misunderstood* Roman Testament. Otherwise it might be said that every achievement of an older period, which is adopted in later times, is part of the *old misunderstood*. For example, the three unities, as the French dramatists under Louis XIV theoretically construe them, most surely rest on a misunderstanding of the Greek drama (and of Aristotle, its exponent). On the other hand, it is equally certain that they understood the Greeks in just such a way as suited their own artistic needs which is why they still clung to this so-called "classical" drama long after Dacier and others had correctly interpreted Aristotle for them. Thus, too, all modern constitutions rest in great part on the *misunderstood* English constitution, for they take as essential precisely that which constitutes the decadence of the English constitution—which now exists only *formally, per abusum,* in England—e.g., a so-called responsible *Cabinet.* The misunderstood form is precisely the general form, applicable for general use at a definite stage of social development

ENGELS, from: Letter to Franz Mehring, July 14, 1893

Today is my first opportunity to thank you for the *Lessing Legend* you were kind enough to send me.* I did not want to reply with a bare formal acknowledgement of receipt of the book but intended at the same time to tell you something about it, about its contents. Hence the delay.

I shall begin at the end—the appendix on historical materialism, in which you have lined up the main things excellently and for any unprejudiced person convincingly. If I find anything to object to, it is that you give me more credit than I deserve, even if I count in everything which I might possibly have found out for myself—in time—but which Marx with his more rapid *coup d'oeil* and wider vision discovered much more quickly. When one has the good fortune to work for forty years with a man like Marx, one does not usually get the recognition one thinks one deserves during his lifetime. Then, if the greater man dies, the lesser easily gets overrated, and this seems to me to be just my case at present; history will set all this right in the end and by that time one will have quietly turned up one's toes and not know anything any more about anything.

Otherwise, there is only one point lacking, which, however, Marx and I always failed to stress enough in our writings and in regard to which we are all equally guilty. That is to say, we all laid, and *were bound* to lay, the main emphasis, in the first place, on the *derivation* of political, juridical and other ideological notions, and of actions arising through the medium of these notions, from basic economic facts. But in so doing we neglected the formal side—the ways and means by which these notions, etc., come about—for the sake of the content. This has given our adversaries a welcome opportunity for misunderstandings and distortions, of which Paul Barth** is a striking example.

Ideology is a process accomplished by the so-called thinker consciously, it is true, but with a false consciousness. The real motive forces impelling him remain unknown to him: otherwise, it simply would not be an ideological process. Hence, he imagines false or seeming motive forces. Because it is a process

---

* Franz Mehring (1846-1919), the major literary critic in the German Social-Democratic Party until his death, published his study of the class-conditioned scholarship on Lessing in 1893.

** Paul Barth (1858-1922), German philosopher and sociologist, professor at the University of Leipzig.

of thought he derives its form as well as its content from pure thought, either his own or that of his predecessors. He works with mere thought material, which he accepts without examination as the product of thought, and does not investigate further for a more remote source independent of thought; indeed, this is a matter of course to him because, as all action is *mediated* by thought, it appears to him to be ultimately *based* upon thought.

The ideologist who deals with history (history is here simply meant to comprise all the spheres—political, juridical, philosophical, theological—belonging to *society* and not only to nature) thus possesses in every sphere of science material which has formed itself independently out of the thought of previous generations and has gone through its own independent process of development in the brains of these successive generations. True, external facts belonging to one or another sphere may have exercised a codetermining influence on this development, but the tacit presupposition is that these facts themselves are also only the fruits of a process of thought, and so we still remain wihin that realm of mere thought, which apparently has successfully digested even the hardest facts.

It is above all this appearance of an independent history of state constitutions, of systems of law, of ideological conceptions in every separate domain that dazzles most people. If Luther and Calvin "overcome" the official Catholic religion or Hegel "overcomes" Fichte and Kant or Rousseau with his republican *contrat social* indirectly overcomes the constitutional Montesquieu, this is a process which remains within theology, philosophy or political science, represents a stage in the history of these particular spheres of thought and never passes beyond the sphere of thought. And since the bourgeois illusion of the eternity and finality of capitalist production has been added as well, even the overcoming of the mercantilists by the physiocrats and Adam Smith is accounted as a sheer victory of thought; not as the reflection in thought of changed economic facts but as the finally achieved correct understanding of actual conditions subsisting always and everywhere—in fact, if Richard Coeur de Lion and Philip Augustus had introduced free trade instead of getting mixed up in the crusades we should have been spared five hundred years of misery and stupidity.

It is this aspect of the matter, which I can only indicate here, that we have all, I think, neglected more than it deserves. It is the same old story: form is always neglected at first for content. As I say, I have done that, too, and the mistake has always struck me only later. So I am not only far from reproaching you with this in any way—as the older of the guilty parties, I certainly have no right to do so. On the contrary. But I would like all the same to draw your attention to this point for the future.

In connection with this is the fatuous notion of the ideologist that, because we deny an independent historical development to the various ideological spheres which play a part in history, we also deny them any *effect upon history*. The basis of this is the common undialectical conception of cause and effect as rigidly opposite poles, the total disregarding of interaction. These gentlemen often (almost deliberately) forget that once a historic element has been brought into the world by other, ultimately economic causes, it reacts, can react on its environment and even on the causes that have given rise to it. For instance, Barth on the priesthood and religion, on your page 475. I was very glad to see how you dealt with this fellow whose banality exceeds all expectation; and him they make professor of history in Leipzig! I must say that old man Wachsmuth—also rather a bonehead but greatly appreciative of facts—was quite a different chap.

As for the rest, I can only repeat about the book what I repeatedly said about the articles when they appeared in the *Neue Zeit:* it is by far the best presentation in existence of the genesis of the Prussian state. Indeed, I may well say that it is the only good presentation, correctly developing in most matters their interconnection down to the smallest details.

ENGELS, from: Letter to Laura Lafargue, September 18, 1893

Yesterday we were in the Freie Volksbühne—the Lessing Theater, one of the nicest and best of Berlin had been hired for the occasion.* The seats are drawn for as in a lottery by the

---

* This letter was written in English by Engels while on his first visit to Germany in forty years. The *Freie Bühne*, 'Free Stage' was founded by Otto Brahm in 1889 to introduce the Naturalistic drama of Ibsen, Zola, Tolstoy, etc., to Berlin and Germany after decades of sterile theatrical production. It inspired the membership-controlled bargain-priced *Freie Volksbühne*, 'Free People's Stage' (1890) organized by people close to the Social-Democratic Party and the trade unions primarily for a working-class audience. Berlin's best directors and actors were hired to perform both in Naturalistic pieces (the play seen by Engels was Hermann Sudermann's *Heimat*) and in plays by Shakespeare, Goethe and Schiller; the latter group proved much the

subscribers and you see working men and girls in the stalls and boxes, while bourgeois may be relegated to the gods. The public is of an attention, a devotion, I might say, an enthusiasm sans égal (without equal). Not a sign of applause until the curtain falls—then a veritable storm. But in pathetic scenes—torrents of tears. No wonder the actors prefer this public to any other. The piece was rather good and the acting far superior to what I had expected. The *Kleinbürgerei* [provincialism] of old has disappeared from the German stage, both in the acting and in the character of the pieces. I will send you a short review of the latter.

more popular owing to their vitality and winning attitude, while of the Naturalistic group, only Hauptmann's *The Weavers* had comparable appeal. F. Mehring analyzed the *Freie Volksbühne* in a notable critique (*Neue Zeit*, October 21, 1896). Engels' 'short review,' if written, does not survive.

THE PROBLEM OF REALISM

MARX, from: "The English Middle Class" (1854)

The present splendid brotherhood of fiction writers in England, whose graphic and eloquent pages have issued to the world more political and social truths than have been uttered by all the professional politicians, publicists and moralists put together, have described every section of the middle class from the "highly genteel" annuitant and fundholder, who looks upon all sorts of business as vulgar, to the little shopkeeper and lawyer's clerk. And how have Dickens and Thackeray, Miss Bronte and Mrs. Gaskell painted them? As full of presumption, affectation, petty tyranny and ignorance; and the civilized world have confirmed their verdict with the damning epigram that it has fixed to this class "that they are servile to those above, and tyrannical to those beneath them."

MARX, from: Letter to Frederick Engels, November 24, 1858

[In the literary weekly published by Robert] Prutz that dolt Ruge has proven that "Shakespeare was no dramatic poet" because he "had no philosophical system," while Schiller, because he was a Kantian, is a *truly* "dramatic poet." In response, Prutz has written a "vindication of Shakespeare!"*

* Arnold Ruge (1802-1880), a Young Hegelian, radical publicist, and political leader, whose activity forced him to emigrate to England for a long time. His essays unfavorably comparing Shakespeare with Schiller were published in honor of the latter's birth centenary.

MARX, from: Letter to Ferdinand Lassalle, April 19, 1859

Secondly: The conflict chosen* is not tragic but is the tragic conflict which unerringly caused the wreck of the revolutionary party in 1848-49.** I can therefore only approve most highly

* Engels is referring to the conflict in Ferdinand Lassalle's play *Franz von Sickingen.*
** The initial part of this letter is separately presented in the section on "Form and Style." Ferdinand Lassalle (1825-1864), a lawyer, author, compelling speaker and brilliant organizer of the German working class, who had known Marx and Engels from the 1848-49 Revolution, wrote the tragedy *Franz von Sickingen* in 1858-59. Sickingen was, with Ulrich von Hutten, the leader of the uprising of Swabian and Rheinland knights in 1522-23 on which the play is based. Sickingen led the knighted nobility against the dukes and above all the

the intention of making it the pivot of a modern tragedy. Yet, I ask myself whether the subject chosen by you is appropriate for the presentation of this conflict. Balthasar*** can actually imagine that, if Sickingen had raised the flag of battle against the emperor and declared open war against the dukes, rather than concealing his revolt beneath a knightly feud, he would have been victorious. But can we share this illusion? Sickingen (and with him Hutten, more or less) did not lose because of his wiles. He went down in defeat because, as a *knight* and a *representative of a perishing class*, he rose up against the existing order or rather against its new form. If you strip away from Sickingen all that pertains to his individuality by way of particular training, natural gifts, etc., then we are left with—Götz von Berlichingen. The tragic opposition of the knighthood against the emperor and the dukes is embodied in this *wretched* figure and given in its appropriate form, and Goethe rightly chose him for the hero. In so far as Sickingen—and even to some extent Hutten, although with respect to him, as with respect to all class ideologists, judgments must be modified considerably—struggles against the dukes (his demarche against the emperor can be explained only by the fact the emperor transforms himself from the emperor of the knights into the emperor of dukes), he is simply a Don Quixote, although historically justified. The fact that he begins the revolt under the guise of a feud among the knights only means that he begins it *as a knight*. If he were to begin it otherwise, he would have to appeal directly and at once to the cities and peasants, that is, to those very classes whose development equals (or means) the negation of knighthood.

If then you did not want to reduce the conflict to the one in *Götz von Berlichingen*—and this was not your intention—Sickingen and Hutten had to perish because in their own imaginations they were revolutionists (which cannot be said of Götz) and, completely like the *educated* Polish nobility of 1830, they made themselves on the one hand into spokesmen of contemporary ideas, and on the other, representatives indeed of reactionary class interests. In this case, then, the *noble* representatives of revolution,—behind whose slogans of unity and liberty the hope of the old imperial power and fistic right is

---

archbishop of Trier; he was killed when the knights abandoned him. On March 6, 1859, Lassalle had sent the playscript to Marx together with an essay outlining the tragic idea underlying the play. *Franz von Sickingen* was translated into English by Daniel DeLeon (1910).

*** Balthasar Stör, Sickingen's servant.

concealed—should not take up all the interest as in your play, but the representatives of the peasantry (especially them) and the revolutionary elements in the cities should have provided an important and active background for your play. Then you could have expressed in much greater measure the most modern ideas in their purest form. As it is the major theme of your play, together with *religious* freedom, remains civil *unity*. You would then have *Shakespearized* more; at present, there is too much *Schillerism*, which means making individuals into mere mouth-pieces of the spirit of the times, and this is your main fault. Did you not, to a certain extent, like your own Franz von Sickingen, make the same diplomatic mistake of setting the Lutheran-knightly opposition higher than the plebian Münzer one?****

In addition, I do not find any characteristic traits in your characters, with the exception of Charles V, Balthasar, and Richard of Trier. And is there any other period with such sharp characters as the XVI century? Your Hutten, to my mind, is much too much a mere representative of "enthusiasm," and this is boring. Wasn't he both pretty clever and a jokester, and wasn't he badly mistreated?

To what extent even your Sickingen (also, by the way, drawn much too abstractly) is the victim of a conflict independent of all his personal calculations can be seen from his finding it necessary to preach to his knights about friendship with the city, etc. and, on the other hand, from how much pleasure it gives him to exercise club-law over the cities.

As to particular points of criticism, you sometimes allow your characters much too much self-reflection—which is due to your preference for Schiller. Thus on page 121, where Hutten is telling Maria his life history, it would have been highly natural to have allowed Maria to say:

"All the gamut of sensations,"
and so on to

"And weightier than load of years it is."
The preceding verses from "They say" to "grown old" could then be made to follow after, but the reflection "A night is all a maiden needs to become a woman" (although it shows that Maria knows more than mere abstract love) was entirely unnecessary; and Maria's beginning discussion of her own "aging" is altogether misplaced. After she has told all that she

---

**** Martin Luther favored a moderate reform, suited to the needs of the lower nobility, the middle class in the cities, and the more advanced dukes. In contrast, Thomas Münzer had urged the end of feudalism. Münzer's peasant army was defeated in May 1525, and he was captured, tortured and killed.

has in the "one" hour, she could express the general feeling of her mood in the sentence on her growing old. Furthermore, I am disturbed by the following lines: "I thought it was a *right*" (i.e., happiness). Why rob Maria of the naive view of the world which she maintains up until that point by turning it into a doctrine of rights? Perhaps I shall be able to give you my opinion in more detail on another occasion.

I think the scene between Sickingen and Charles V very good, although the dialogue on both sides comes to sound more like lawyers holding forth in court; the scenes in Trier are also very good. Hutten's speech on the sword is excellent.

But enough for now.

In the person of my wife you have won a warm adherent of your drama. Only she is not satisfied with Maria.

Salut

K.M.

ENGELS, from: Letter to Ferdinand Lassalle, May 18, 1859

With regard to the historical content,* you have presented the two sides of the movement of that time which were most important for you, and in such a way that they are quite obvious and justifiably pertinent to subsequent developments of the national movement of the nobility, represented by Sickingen, and the humanistic-theoretical movement with its later development in the area of the church and theology—the Reformation. The best scenes here are between Sickingen and the emperor, between the papal legate and the archbishop of Trier (here you have succeeded in rendering excellent individual characterizations in the antithesis between the worldly legate, educated in the classics and aesthetics, politically and theoretically far-seeing, and the narrow-minded German duke of the priests, and they follow distinctly from the *representative* characters of the persons); the characterization in the scene between Sickingen and Charles is also very striking. With Hutten's autobiography, the *contents* of which you justly consider essential, you chose a very risky means of inserting this content in the drama. The dialogue between Franz and Balthasar in the

---

* The first part of this letter is presented in the section on "Form and Style."

fifth act, in which the latter tells his master of the *genuinely revolutionary* policy he should have followed is also of great importance. Here is where the genuine tragedy becomes apparent, and precisely because of its significance, I feel it should have been more strongly suggested in the third act where there were more opportunities to do so. But I am slipping back again into secondary matters.—The standpoint of the cities and of the dukes of that time is also presented very clearly in several places, and thus, the so-to-speak *official* elements of the movement of that time are nearly exhausted. It seems to me, however, that you have not paid sufficient attention to the unofficial, plebeian, and peasant elements with their concomitant theoretical representation. The peasant movement was in its way just as national, just as opposed to the dukes as was the movement of the nobility, and the colossal dimensions of the struggle in which the peasants succumbed stand in great contrast to the ease with which the nobility, leaving Sickingen to his fate, acquiesced again in its historical role of court servility. Therefore, it seems to me that even with your conception of the drama which is, as you now see, to my mind somewhat too abstract and insufficiently realistic, the peasant movement deserved more attention. To be sure, the peasant scene with Jost Fritz is characteristic, and the individuality of this "agitator" is rendered very correctly, but in contraposition to the nobility movement, it does not represent adequately the peasant agitation which by then had already increased to its boiling point. In *my* view of drama, the realistic should not be neglected in favor of the intellectual elements, nor Shakespeare in favor of Schiller. Had you introduced the wonderfully variegated plebian social sphere of that time, it would have lent entirely new material which would have enlivened and provided an indispensible background for the action being played out on the forestage by the national movement of the nobility and it would at last have thrown proper light on this very movement. What wonderfully distinctive character portraits are to be found during this period of the breakdown of feudalism—penniless ruling kings, impoverished hireling soldiers and adventurers of all sorts—a Falstaffian background that, in an historical play of *this* type, would be much more effective than in Shakespeare! But, aside from this, it seems to me that the neglect of the peasant movement has led you in one respect to draw even the nationalist movement of the nobility incorrectly, and the *real* tragic element in Sickingen's fate has escaped you. In my opinion, the majority of the imperial aristocracy at that time did not think of forming an alliance with the peasantry; their dependence on the income from the oppressed peasantry did not permit this. An alliance with the cities was more feasible; but this was never realized or was realized only very partially. Yet, the success of the national revolution of the nobility was possible only through an alliance with the cities and peasantry, especially the latter; and this, to my mind, was the tragic circumstance, that the basic condition, an alliance with the peasantry was impossible, that the policy of the nobility had necessarily to be trivial, that at the very moment when it wished to represent the national movement, the masses of the nation, the peasantry, protested against its leadership, and so it necessarily had to fall. I have no means of judging in how far you are historically correct in assuming that Sickingen was in some way really associated with the peasantry, nor is this of much importance. By the way, as far as I remember, Hutten's writings, where he appeals to the peasantry, carefully avoid this ticklish question of the nobility and attempt to direct all the anger of the peasants against the priests. However, I do not in the least take issue against your right to portray Sickingen and Hutten as if they had intended to liberate the peasants. But here you had at once the tragic contradiction: they both stood between a nobility decidedly *opposed to this* on the one side, and the peasantry on the other. In my opinion, this constituted the tragic conflict between the historically necessary postulate and the practical impossibility of its realization. When you let this moment slip, you reduce the tragic conflict to lesser dimensions, setting Sickingen immediately against only *one* duke and not against the emperor and empire (although you do bring in the peasants here at the right moment), and he perishes, according to you, simply on account of the indifference and cowardliness of the nobles. But this would have been grounded altogether differently if you had stressed the growing wrath of the peasantry earlier as well as the definitely more conservative mood of the nobility as a result of the previous peasant "Bundschuhe" and "Armer Konrad" ** rebellions. This is only one of many ways in which it would be possible to introduce the peasant and plebeian movements into the drama; there are at least ten other ways just as conceivable or more so.

As you see, I approach your work with very high criteria—in fact the *highest* from an aesthetic and historical viewpoint—and

** The *Bundschuh* and *Armer Konrad* were the greatest peasant rebel movements. They had developed as early as 1514, and they triggered the Peasant War of 1525-26.

if I have to do this to make objections, it is proof of my recognition of your work. *Mutual* criticism has long, in the interests of the party, assumed as candid a character as possible. On the whole, it always gives me and all of us pleasure to find new proof that whatever field the party enters, it always shows its superiority. And that is what you have done this time also.

MARX, from: Letter to Nannette Philips, March 24, 1861

I arrived at Berlin on Sunday last (18th March), at 7 o'clock in the morning. My travel was not marked by any incident save a 6½ hours' delay at Oberhausen, an abominably tedious little place. Lassalle, who lives in a very fine house, situated in one of the finest streets of Berlin, had everything prepared for my reception, and gave me a most friendly welcome. The first hours having been talked away and my railway-fatigue chased by some rest and some refreshment, Lassalle introduced me at once to the house of the Countess of Hatzfeldt who, as I soon became aware, dines every day in his house at 4 o'clock p.m., and passes her evenings with him. I found her hair as "blonde" and her eyes as blue as formerly, but for the remainder of her face I read the words imprinted on it: twenty and twenty make fifty-seven. There were in fact wrinkles full of "vestiges of creation," there were cheeks and chin betraying an embonpoint which, like coal beds, want much time to be formed, and so forth. As to her eyebrows, I was at once struck by the circumstance that they had improved instead of deteriorating, so that art had by far got the better of nature. On later occasions I made the general remark that she perfectly understands the art of making herself up and of finding in her toilette-box the tints no longer derived from her blood. Upon the whole she reminded me of some Greek statues which still boast of fine bust but whose heads have been cruelly "beknappered" by the vicissitudes of time. Still, to be not unjust, she is a very distinguished lady, no blue-stocking, of great natural intellect, much vivacity, deeply interested in the revolutionary movement, and of an aristocratic *laissez allez* very superior to the pedantic grimaces of professional *femmes d'esprit*....

On Tuesday evening Lassalle and the countess led me to a Berlin theatre where a Berlin comedy, full of Prussian self-glorification, was exacted. It was altogether a disgusting affair. On Wednesday evening I was forced by them to assist at the performance of a ballet in the opera house. We had a box for ourselves at the side—*horrible dictu*—of the king's "loge." Such a ballet is characteristic of Berlin. It forms not, as at Paris, or at London, an *entrejeu*, or the conclusion, of an opera, but it absorbs the whole evening, is divided into several acts, etc. Not a syllable is spoken by the actors, but everything is hinted at by mimickry. It is in fact deadly—dully. The scenery, however, was beautiful; you assisted for instance at a sea-voyage from Livorno to Naples; sea, mountains, seacoast, towns etc., everything being represented with photographical truth.

ENGELS, from: Letter to Laura Lafargue, December 13, 1883

By the bye I have been reading nothing but Balzac while laid up, and enjoyed the grand old fellow thoroughly. *There* is the history of France from 1815 to 1848, far more than in all the Valulabelles, Capefigues, Louis Blancs *et tutti quanti* [all the rest of them]. And what boldness! What a revolutionary dialectic in his poetical justice!

ENGELS, from: Letter to Minna Kautsky, November 26, 1885

I have read *The Old and the New*, for which I am heartily grateful to you.* The life of the workers of the salt diggings is described in just such a masterly way as the life of the peasants in *Stefan*. Also most of the scenes of Viennese society are very good. Vienna indeed is the only German city where there is any society; in Berlin, there are only "certain circles," and still more uncertain ones, and it therefore offers a basis only for novels about the literati, bureaucrats and actors. Whether the motivation of the action in this part of your work does not develop a little too hastily is easier for you to judge than for me. Much of what produces such an impression on us may be perfectly natural in Vienna, with its own sort of international character, full of southern and eastern European elements. The characters in both milieus are drawn with your usual precision of individualization. Each person is a type, but at the same time

* *Die Alten und die Neuen*, the novel here discussed by Engels, appeared in the periodical *Die neue Welt* in 1884. Minna Kautsky (1837-1912), the mother of Karl Kautsky, was well-known to the Social-Democratic movement for her social novels and stories. *Stefan vom Grillenhof* was her first novel, published in the same journal five years earlier.

a distinct personality, *ein dieser*** as old Hegel would say. That is as it should be. But to be properly nonpartisan I must set out to find something wrong, and here I come to Arnold. In truth, he is too faultless, and, if at last he perishes by falling from a mountain, one can reconcile this with poetic justice only by saying that he was too good for this world. It is always bad for for an author to be infatuated with his hero, and it seems to me that in this case you have somewhat succumbed to this weakness. Elsa still has traces of personality, although she is also idealized, but in Arnold personality is dissolved in principle.

The root of this defect is indicated, by the way, in the novel itself. Evidently you felt the need in this book to declare publicly for your party, to bear witness before the whole world and show your convictions. Now you have done this; you have it behind you and have no need to do so again in this form. I am not at all an opponent of tendentious writing [*Tendenzpoesie*] as such. The father of tragedy, Aeschulus, and the father of comedy, Aristophanes, were both strong tendentious poets, as were Dante and Cervantes, and the main merit of Schiller's *Love and Intrigue* [Kabale und Liebe] is that it is the first German political tendentious drama [*Tendenzdrama*]. Contemporary Russian and Norweigian authors, who are writing superlative novels, are all tendentious. But I believe the tendency must spring forth from the situation and the action itself, without explicit attention called to it; the writer is not obliged to offer to the reader the future historical solution of the social conflicts he depicts. Especially in our conditions, the novel primarily finds readers in bourgeois circles, circles not directly related to our own, and there the socialist tendentious novel can fully achieve its purpose, in my view, if, by conscientiously describing the real mutual relations, it breaks down the conventionalized illusions dominating them, shatters the optimism of the bourgeois world, causes doubt about the eternal validity of the existing order, and this without directly offering a solution or even, under some circumstances, taking an ostensible partisan stand. Your exact knowledge both of the Austrian peasantry and of Viennese "society" and your marvelous freshness in depicting them here provide a great quantity of material, while in *Stefan* you proved that you knew how to manage your heroes with that fine irony which demonstrates the mastery of the writer over his creation.

** "This one."

ENGELS, from: Letter to Margaret Harkness, Beginning of April 1888 (draft)

Dear Miss H[arkness],

I thank you very much for sending me through Messrs. Vizetelly your *City Girl*.* I have read it with the greatest pleasure and avidity. It is, indeed, as my friend Eichhoff your translator calls it, *ein kleines Kunstwerk* [a small work of art]; to which he adds, what will be satisfactory to you, that consequently his translation must be all but literal, as any omission or attempted manipulation could only destroy part of the original's value.

What strikes me most in your tale besides its realistic truth is that it exhibits the courage of the true artist. Not only in the way you treat the Salvation Army, in the teeth of supercilious respectability, which respectability will perhaps learn from your tale, for the first time, *why* the Salvation Army has such a hold on the popular masses. But chiefly in the plain unvarnished manner in which you make the old, old story, the proletarian girl seduced by a middle class man, the pivot of the whole book. Mediocrity would have felt bound to hide the, to it, commonplace character of the plot under heaps of artificial complications and adornments, and yet would not have got rid of the fate of being found out. You felt you could afford to tell an old story, because you could make it a new one by simply telling it truly.

Your Mr. Arthur Grant is a masterpiece.

If I have anything to criticise, it would be that perhaps after all, the tale is not quite realistic enough. Realism, to my mind, implies, besides truth of detail, the truthful reproduction of typical characters under typical circumstances. Now your characters are typical enough, as far as they go; but the circumstances which surround them and make them act, are not perhaps equally so. In the "City Girl" the working class figures as a passive mass, unable to help itself and not even making any attempt at striving to help itself. All attempts to

* * *

* *A City Girl: A Realistic Story* appeared in 1887. Margaret Harkness published several novels on English working-class life under the pseudonym John Law. A friend of Marx's daughter Eleanor, she had lived in Engels' house and was a member of the Social Democratic Federation. Engels thought *A City Girl* and her subsequent *Out of Work* were useful socialist literature, and he asked the German writer Wilhelm Eichhoff, mentioned here, to translate them both. Engels wrote this draft of his letter to Harkness in English.

drag it out of its torpid misery come from without, from above. Now if this was a correct description about 1800 or 1810, in the days of Saint Simon and Robert Owen, it cannot appear so in 1887 to a man who for nearly fifty years has had the honour of sharing in most of the fights of the militant proletariat. The rebellious reaction of the working class against the oppressive medium which surrounds them, their attempts—convulsive, half-conscious or conscious—at recovering their status as human beings, belong to history and must therefore lay claim to a place in the domain of realism.

I am far from finding fault with your not having written a point blank socialist novel, a "Tendenzroman" as we Germans call it, to glorify the social and political views of the author. That is not at all what I mean. The more the opinions of the author remain hidden, the better for the work of art. The realism I allude to, may crop out even in spite of the author's opinions. Let me refer to an example. Balzac whom I consider a far greater master of realism than all the Zolas *passés, présents et à venir*, [past, present, and future] in *La Comédie humaine* gives us a most wonderfully realistic history of French "Society," describing, chronicle-fashion, almost year by year from 1816 to 1848, the progressive inroads of the rising bourgeoisie upon the society of nobles, that reconstituted itself after 1815 and that set up again, as far as it could, the standard of *la vieille politesse française* [the old French ways]. He describes how the last remnants of this, to him, model society gradually succumbed before the intrusion of the vulgar moneyed upstart, or were corrupted by him; how the grande dame whose conjugal infidelities were but a mode of asserting herself in perfect accordance with the way she had been disposed of in marriage, gave way to the bourgeoise, who corned her husband for cash or cashmere; and around this central picture he groups a complete history of French Society from which, even in economical details (for instance the re-arrangement of real and personal property after the Revolution) I have learned more than from all the professed historians, economists and statisticians of the period together. Well, Balzac was politically a Legitimist; his great work is a constant elegy on the irretrievable decay of good society; his sympathies are all with the class doomed to extinction. But for all that his satyre is never keener, his irony never bitterer than when he sets in motion the very men and women with whom he sympathises most deeply—the nobles. And the only men of whom he always speaks with undisguised admiration, are his bitterest political antagonists, the republican heroes of the Cloître Saint Merri

[*Méry*], the men, who at that time (1830-36) were indeed the representatives of the popular masses.** That Balzac thus was compelled to go against his own class sympathies and political prejudices, that he *saw* the necessity of the downfall of his favorite nobles, and described them as people deserving no better fate; and that he *saw* the real men of the future where, for the time being, they alone were to be found—that I consider one of the greatest triumphs of Realism, and one of the grandest features of old Balzac.

I must own, in your defence, that nowhere in the civilized world are the working people less actively resistent, more passively submitting to fate, more *hébétés* [dulled] than in the East End of London. And how do I know whether you have not had very good reasons for contenting yourself, for once, with a picture of the passive side of working class life, reserving the active side for another work?

** Next to this cloister, on June 5-6, 1832, the leftwing supporters of the Republican party fought a last-ditch battle on the barricades against the troops of Louis-Philippe.

TENDENCY LITERATURE

MARX, from: *The Holy Family*, 1845

As bad painters must label their painting to say what it is supposed to represent, Eugène Sue must put a label in *"bull-dog" Chourineur's* mouth so that he constantly affirms: "The two words, 'You still have heart and honor,' made a *man* out of me."* Till his very last breath *Chourineur* will find the motives for his actions, not in his human individuality, but in that label. As a proof of his moral amendment he will often reflect on his own excellence and the wickedness of other individuals. And every time he throws about moralizing expressions, Rudolph will say to him: "i like to hear you *speak* like that." *Chourineur* has not become an ordinary *bull-dog* but a *moral one*....

The most wretched offal of socialist literature, a sample of which we find in this novelist, reveal "mysteries" still unknown to Critical Criticism.

* The discussion concerns Sue's novel *The Mysteries of Paris*.

ENGELS, from: *The New York Daily Tribune*, October 28, 1851

The political movement of the middle class or bourgeoisie, in Germany, may be dated from 1840. It had been preceded by symptoms showing that the moneyed and industrial class of that country was ripening into a state which would no longer allow it to continue apathetic and passive under the pressure of a half-feudal, half-bureaucratic Monarchism....

German literature, too, laboured under the influence of the political excitement into which all Europe had been thrown by the events of 1830. A crude Constitutionalism, or a still cruder Republicanism, were preached by almost all writers of the time. It became more and more the habit, particularly of the inferior sorts of literati, to make up for the want of cleverness in their productions, by political allusions which were sure to attract attention. Poetry, novels, reviews, the drama, every literary production teemed with what was called "tendency", that is with more or less timid exhibitions of an anti-governmental spirit. In order to complete the confusion of ideas reigning after 1830 in Germany, with these elements of political opposition there were mixed up ill-digested university-recollections of German philosophy, and misunderstood gleanings from French Socialism, particularly Saint-Simonism; and the clique of writers who expatiated upon this heterogeneous conglomerate of ideas, presumptiously called themselves "Young Germany," or "the Modern School." They have since repented their youthful sins, but not improved their style of writing.*

* In the section on "Form and Style" we print a letter from Engels to Wilhelm Gräber of October 8, 1839, which shows Engels at age nineteen still enthusiastic about entering the "Modern School" of writing. However, as early as June 1842, in a book review of Alexander Jung's *Vorlesungen über die moderne Literatur der Deutschen* [Lectures on Modern German Literature], Engels adopted a position similar to that of 1851-52 printed above. Bitingly, he attacked Jung (1799-1884) for categorizing the 'beauties' of the Young Germany style while having no understanding of its political implications: "He has learned nothing, forgotten nothing. The Young Germany movement has passed, the Young Hegelian movement has emerged; Strauss, Feuerbach, Bauer and the *Jahrbücher* have drawn widespread attention; the struggle over principles is at its height, a life-and-death confrontation with Christianity the bone of argument; the political movement spreads everywhere, and good old Jung still naively thinks the 'Nation' has nothing better to do than await a new play by Gutzkow, a promising novel by Mundt, or something predictably eccentric by Laub. All Germany resounds with the cries of struggle, the new principles are debated at his very feet, and Mr. Jung sits in his neat little room, chews upon a pen, and broods over the concept of the 'Modern'."

MARX, from: Letter to Joseph Weydemeyer, January 16, 1852

I am enclosing a poem and a private letter by Freiligrath.* Now I ask you to: (1) Have the poem printed carefully; the stanzas separated at adequate intervals, and the whole thing printed without an eye to saving space. Poetry loses much when the verses are printed all crowded together. (2) Write a friendly letter to Freiligrath. Don't be afraid to compliment him, for all poets, even the best of them, are *plus ou moins des courtisanes, et il faut les cajoler, pour les faire chanter* [courtesans, more or less, and they have to be cajoled to make them sing]. Our F[reiligrath] is the kindest, most unassuming man in private life, who conceals *un esprit très fin et très railleur* [a very subtle and mocking spirit] underneath his genuine simplicity, and whose pathos is "genuine" without making him "uncritical" and superstitious." He is a real revolutionary and an honest

* Ferdinand Freiligrath (1810-1876), German revolutionary poet, member of the editorial committee of *Neue Rheinische Zeitung* and the Communist League (*Bund der Kommunisten*); and Joseph Weydemeyer (1818-1886). Communist League member and 1848er who emigrated in 1851 to the U.S., where he started the magazine *Revolution*.

man through and through—praise that I would not mete out to many. Nevertheless, a poet—no matter what he may be as a man—requires applause, admiration. I think it lies in the very nature of the species. I am telling you all this merely to call your attention to the fact that in your correspondence with Freiligrath you must not forget the difference between a "poet" and a "critic." Moreover, it is very nice of him to address his poetic letter directly to you. I think this will give you something by way of contrast in New York.

MARX, from: Letter to Frederick Engels, May 8, 1856

Appros! I've seen Heine's Testament!* Return to the "living God" and an "Apology Before God and Man" if anything he ever wrote was "immoral," this is it!

* Heinrich Heine (1797-1856), the most important pre-1848 German political poet; widely considered to rank among the great nineteenth-century authors. For the friendship of Heine and Marx, see the Supplement.

MARX, from: Letter to Ferdinand Freiligrath, February 29, 1860

Of the "party" in the sense of your letter I have known *nothing* since 1852...*

I have openly told you my view, which I hope you share in essentials. I have further tried to dispell the misunderstanding that I mean by "party," a *Bund* now eight years dead or a newspaper editorial committee dissolved twelve years ago. By party I have understood the party in the great historical sense.

* Ferdinand Freiligrath was an editor of the *Neue Rheinische Zeitung* in 1848-49 when Marx was chief editor. Marx wrote these words when a break of personal ties between himself and Freiligrath seemed imminent. It was triggered when a friend of G. Kinkel, a politically liberal German poet living in exile in London, to whom Freiligrath had grown closer, published an article in praise of Freiligrath, in which Marx's dark influence was claimed to have nearly destroyed the poet's talent. Marx responded to this in a letter to Freiligrath of November 23, 1859: "If one wanted *wrongly* to ascribe to me any influence on you, this could have been only in the brief period of the *Neue Rheinische Zeitung*, when you wrote your very famous and certainly most popular poems." The immediate reason for Marx's paragraph on the party in "the great historical sense" was a letter to him of the day before, in which Freiligrath wrote, among other things: "Although I have always remained true to the banner of the *classe la plus laborieuse et la plus* *misérable* and always will, you know as well as I do that my relationship to the Party as it was and to the Party as it is are of a different nature. When the *Bund* was dissolved at the end of 1852 as the result of the Cologne Trials, I laid aside all the bonds which the party as such laid on me, and maintained only a personal relationship to *you*, my friend and comrade in *conscience*. For these seven years I have stood far from the *party*. I have not attended its meetings, I have been unaware of its decisions and acts. Thus my relationship to the party was long ago dissolved, we have never deceived one another about this, it was a kind of tacit convention between us. And I can only say that I have felt good about it. My nature and that of every poet needs freedom! The party, too, is a cage, and one can 'sing' better, even *for* the party, outside than in. I was a poet of the proletariat and the revolution long before I was a member of the *Bund* and member of the editorial committee of the *Neue Rheinische Zeitung*! So I will continue to stand on my own feet, I will hearken only to myself, and I will answer for myself!" The earliest analysis of the Freiligrath declaration and response by Marx was provided by Franz Mehring ("Freiligrath und Marx in ihrem Briefwechsel," *Neue Zeit*, April 12, 1912). This remains a most satisfactory interpretation.

MARX, from: Letter to Frederick Engels, May 29, 1863

As for Itzig [Ferdinand Lassalle], he has urged Freiligrath—Freiligrath told this to me in confidence (and showed me Itzig's letter)—to write *a poem* about the "new" movement [the *Allgemeine Deutsche Arbeiterverein*, headed by Lassalle], in other words to sing Itzig's praise. But he made a bad mistake in picking Freiligrath. Among other things he says in the letter: "Hundreds of newspapers carry my name daily to the farthest corner of Germany." "*My* proletarians! etc." Since Freiligrath has not sung him, he has found another poet. Here is a sample:

Come hither, German *Proletariat*!
Come hither, heed this time a fruitful counsel!
A man stands here prepared to lead the way to
Your own best welfare. Now prepare to *act*!
He has no seat in distant parliaments,
And does not preen upon his speaking talents;
Simple and clear, the Tribune of us all,
The man of the people, *Ferdinand Lassalle*!

Why should you work to fill the purse of *others*
Until your sweat rolls off into the earth,
Why should you live in rags and know but dearth
While *they* grow richer with each passing hour?
The fruits of labor should be *yours* to sample,
The blessings of the soil for *you* be ample,

Oh may by every ear be heard the call:
The manly words of *Ferdinand Lassalle*.

Macte puer [Hail stripling]! If that's not a doggerel for lice!

ENGELS, from: Letter to Karl Marx, December 21, 1866

The old Horace* reminds me in places of Heine, who learned a great deal from him, and also was at bottom an equally ordinary hound in the political sense. One thinks of the honest obedient citizen who dared to risk *vultus instantis tyranni* [the threatening glance of the angry tyrant] only to lick the backside of Augustus. Yet, in other respects the old wretch is very lovable.

* Quintus Horatius Flaccus (65-8 B.C.), a major Roman poet.

ENGELS, from: Letter to Eduard Bernstein, August 17, 1881

You must not heap such compliments on Vallès.* He is a dilettante or, even worse, a miserable phrasemaker and a worthless fellow who, due to lack of talent, has gone to extremes with tendentious junk to show his convictions, but it is really in order to gain an audience. In the Commune he only talked big, and if he had any effect at all, it was detrimental. You should not let your Parisian comradeship (for which Malon too has a soft spot) tie you to this *drôle de fanfaron*, this foolish loudmouth.

* Jules-Louis-Joseph Vallès (1832-1885), French politician, author and journalist. A Proudhonist and member of the International Workingmen's Association, Vallès took part in the Paris Commune, then emigrated to England and later Belgium, before returning to France with the 1880 amnesty of Communards.

ENGELS, "Georg Weerth" (1883)

Song of the Journeyman

Nearby the cherry blossoms
We found a place to stay,
Nearby the cherry blossoms
In Frankfurt did we stay.

The innkeeper did say:
"You're wearing shabby coats!"
"You lousy innkeeper,
'Tis none of your affair!

"Give us some of your wine,
Give us some of your beer;
Give us both beer and wine
And roast some meat for us."

Then the tap creaks in the barrel.
The goodly beer flows out.
It tastes in our mouth
Like urine—just about.

He brought us then a rabbit
With parsley leaves and cabbage;
Before this dead rabbit
We trembled in great fear.

And when we were in bed
Our prayers told for the night,
The bedbugs came at us
The whole night through.

That happened once in Frankfurt,
In lovely Frankfurt town,
He knows it who has lived there
And who has suffered there.

I have found this poem by our friend Weerth* among the
literary remains of Marx. Weerth, the first and most important

* Georg Weerth (1822-1856) was a member of the Communist
League and a friend of both Marx and Engels. Marx had intended such
an article in 1856; Engels published this reminiscence in the *Sozialdemokrat* of June 7, 1883. The poem by Weerth is entitled *Handwerks-
burschenlied* (*Song of the Journeyman*) and was written in 1846.

poet of the German proletariat, was born in Detmold of a Rhineland family. His father was a church superintendent there. When I resided in Manchester in 1843, Weerth came to Bradford as salesman for a German firm, and we spent many a lively Sunday together. In 1845, when Marx and I lived in Brussels, Weerth took over the continental agency for his firm and arranged things so that his headquarters could also be in Brussels. After the March Revolution of 1848, we were all together in Cologne where we founded the *Neue Rheinische Zeitung*. Weerth became the *feuilleton* editor [cultural editor], and I doubt whether any other paper ever had as gay and incisive a *feuilleton*. One of his chief works was "The Life and Deeds of the Famous Knight Schnapphahnski," describing the adventures of Prince Lichnowski, dubbed thus by Heine in his *Atta Troll*. All the facts are true—how we got them will perhaps be told some other time. These Schnapphahnski *feuilletons* were made into an anthololgy and published in 1849 by Hoffmann and Campe. They are still very amusing. Schnapphahnski-Lichnowski met his death on September 18, 1848, in the following manner: with the Prussian General von Auerswald (likewise a member of Parliament), he rode out with a column of peasants to spy on the Frankfurt barricade fighters. The peasants killed both him and von Auerswald as spies, a fate they deserved. But then the German imperial vice-regency filed charges against Weerth for having insulted the dead Lichnowski. Weerth, who had been living in England for some time was sentenced to three months' imprisonment, long after the editorial board of the *Neue Rheinische Zeitung* had been dissolved. Since he had to visit Germany on business from time to time, he actually served this sentence.

In 1850-51, he traveled to Spain, the West Indies, and throughout most of South America as representative of another Bradford firm. After a brief visit to Europe he returned to his beloved West Indies. There he could not forego the pleasure of gazing at least once upon the real original of Louis Napoleon III, the Negro King Soulouque of Haiti. But, as Wilhelm Wolff wrote to Marx on August 28, 1856, he "had difficulties with the quarantine authorities, had to give up his project, and on his tour picked up the germs of yellow fever, which he brought with him to Havana. He got into bed, suffered a cerebral hemorrhage and, on July 30, our Weerth died in Havana."

I called him the first and *most important* poet of the German proletariat. Indeed, his socialist and political poems are far superior to Freiligrath's in originality, wit, and particularly in sensuous fire. He often used Heine-like forms, but clothed them with very original and personal content. And he differed from most poets in that he was completely indifferent to his poems once he wrote them. If he sent a copy of a poem to Marx or myself, he let it go at that, and it often took a great deal of persuading to have him publish it somewhere. Only during the life of the *Neue Rheinische Zeitung* did he behave differently. The reason why is contained in the following excerpt of a letter from Weerth to Marx (dated Hamburg, April 28, 1851):

"By the way, I hope to see you again in London at the beginning of July, for I can't stand these grasshoppers in Hamburg any longer. I am threatened here with a brilliant livelihood, but I am fearful of it. Anyone would grab it with both hands. But I'm too old to become a philistine, and beyond the ocean lies the Far West...

"I have written all sorts of things recently but have finished nothing, for I see no purpose, no end in my scribbling. When *you* write something about political economy, it has meaning and sense. But *me*? To make poor puns and bad jokes for the sake of a silly smile from our grotesque countrymen—really, I know of nothing more pitiful! My writing activity definitely broke down with the end of the *Neue Rheinische Zeitung*.

"I must confess: no matter how sorry I feel that I have wasted away the last three years doing nothing, I'm happy when I think of our paper in Cologne. We did *not* compromise ourselves. That's the main thing! Since Frederick the Great no one has treated the German people so sharply as we did in the *Neue Rheinische Zeitung*.

"I don't mean to say that this was due to me; but I was there....

"O Portugal! O Spain! (W. had just arrived from there.) If we only had your bright skies, your wine, your oranges and myrtle! But we haven't that either! Nothing but rain and long noses and smoked meat!

"In the rain and with a long nose, sincerely

G. Weerth"

There was one thing in which Weerth was unsurpassable, and here he was more masterful than Heine (because he was healthier and less artificial), and only Goethe in the German language excelled him here: that was in expressing natural robust sensuousness and the joys of the flesh. Many readers of the *Sozialdemokrat* would be horrified, were I to reprint here the individual *feuilletons* of the *Neue Rheinische Zeitung*. But I haven't the slightest intention of doing so. Yet, I cannot refrain from pointing out that there will come a time when German Socialists, too, will triumphantly discard the last traces of German philistine prejudices and hypocritical moral prudery— and anyhow, they only serve as a cover for surreptitious obscenity. Read Freiligrath's "Epistles," for instance—you would really think people had no sexual organs. And yet, nobody was more delighted with a quiet bit of smut than Freiligrath, who is so ultra-chaste in his poetry. It is high time that at least the German workers get accustomed to speaking in a free and easy manner as do the peoples of the Romanic lands, Homer and Plato, Horace and Juvenal, the Old Testament, and the *Neue Rheinische Zeitung*, about the things they themselves do every day or night, these natural, indispensible and highly pleasurable things.

Moreover, Weerth has also written less objectionable things, and I am going to take the liberty from time to time of sending some of these pieces to the *feuilleton* of the *Sozialdemokrat*.

ENGELS, Letter to Hermann Schlüter, May 15, 1885

Dear Mr. Schlüter:

As for the poems:*

The *Marseillaise* of the Peasant War was: *Eine feste Burg ist unser Gott* [*A Mighty Fortress is Our God*], and conscious of victory as the text and melody of this song are, it cannot and need not be taken in this sense today. Other songs of the time are to be found in collections of folksongs: *Des Knaben Wunderhorn*, and the like. More may perhaps be found there. But the mercenary soldier largely pre-empted our folk poetry even then.

Of foreign songs I know only the pretty Danish song of *Herr Tidmann*, which I translated in the Berlin *Social-Democrat* [No. 18, February 5, 1865] in 1865.

There were all sorts of Chartist songs, but they aren't to be had any more. One began:

* During the period of anti-Socialist laws in Germany, a Social-Democratic press operated for the German party in Switzerland planned to issue six volumes of revolutionary poetry. Schlüter, for the press, wrote to Engels inquiring whether he knew about several kinds of verse desired for the project, and this was Engels' reply.

Britannia's sons, though slaves you be,
God your creator made you free;
To all he life and freedom gave,
But never, never made a slave.

I don't know any others.
All that has vanished, nor was this poetry worth much.
In 1848 there were two songs sung to the same melody:

1. "Schleswig-Holstein."
2. "The Hecker Song":

Hecker, hoch dein Name schalle
An dem ganzen deutschen Rhein.
Deine Grossmut, ja dein Auge
Flössen schon Vertrauen ein.
Hecker, der als deutscher Mann
Vor der Freiheit sterben kann.

I think that's enough. Then the variant:

Hecker, Struve, Blenker, Zitz und Blum,
Bringt die deitsche Ferschte um!

In general, the poetry of past revolutions (the *Marseillaise* always excepted) rarely has a revolutionary effect for later times because it must also reproduce the mass prejudices of the period in order to affect the masses. Hence the religious nonsense even among the Chartists....

Yours,

F. Engels

THE EXPRESSION AND ENDURANCE
OF FUNDAMENTAL HUMAN VALUES

MARX, from: *Economic and Philosophic Manuscripts of 1844*

It will be seen how the history of *industry* and the established *objective* existence of industry are the *open* book of *man's essential powers*, the exposure to the senses of human *psychology*. Hitherto this was not conceived in its inseparable connection with man's *essential being*, but only in an external relation of utility, because, moving in the realm of estrangement, people could only think man's general mode of being—religion or history in its abstract-general character as politics, art, literature, etc.,—to be the reality of man's essential powers and *man's species-activity*. We have before us the *objectified essential powers* of man in the form of *sensuous, alien, useful objects*, in the form of estrangement, displayed in *ordinary material industry* (which can be conceived as a part of that general movement, just as that movement can be conceived as a particular part of industry, since all human activity hitherto has been labor—that is, industry—activity estranged from itself).

A *psychology* for which this, the part of history most contemporary and accessible to sense, remains a closed book, cannot become a genuine, comprehensive and *real* science. What indeed are we to think of a science which *airily* abstracts from this large part of human labor and which fails to feel its own incompleteness, while such a wealth of human endeavor unfolded before it means nothing more to it than, perhaps, what can be expressed in one word—*"need,"* *"vulgar need"*?

The *natural sciences* have developed an enormous activity and have accumulated a constantly growing mass of material. Philosophy, however, has remained just as alien to them as they remain to philosophy. Their momentary unity was only a *chimerical illusion*. The will was there, but the means were lacking. Even historiography pays regard to natural science only occasionally, as a factor of enlightenment and utility arising from individual great discoveries. But natural science has invaded and transformed human life all the more *practically* through the medium of industry; and has prepared human emancipation, however directly and much it had to consummate dehumanization. *Industry* is the *actual*, historical relation of nature, and therefore of natural science, to man. If, therefore, industry is conceived as the *exoteric* revelation of man's *essential powers*, we also gain an understanding of the *human* essence of nature or the *natural* essence of man. In consequence, natural science will lose its abstractly material— or, rather, its idealistic—tendency, and will become the basis of *human* science, as it has already become the basis of actual human life, albeit in an estranged form. *One* basis for life and another basis for *science* is *a priori* a lie. The nature which comes to be in human history—the genesis of human society—is man's *real* nature; hence nature as it comes to be through industry, even though in an *estranged* form, is true *anthropological* nature.

MARX, from: *Economic and Philosophic Manuscripts of 1844*

In order to abolish the *idea* of private property, the *idea* of communism is completely sufficient. It takes *actual* communist action to abolish actual private property. History will come to it; and this movement, which in *theory* we already know to be a self-transcending movement, will constitute *in actual fact* a very severe and protracted process. But we must regard it as a real advance to have gained beforehand a consciousness of the limited character as well as of the goal of this historical movement—and a consciousness which reaches out beyond it.

When communist *workmen* associate with one another, theory, propaganda, etc., is their first end. But at the same time, as a result of this association, they acquire a new need— the need for society—and what appears as a means becomes an end. You can observe this practical process in its most splendid results whenever you see French socialist workers together. Such things as smoking, drinking, eating, etc., are no longer means of contact or means that bring together. Company, association, and conversation, which again has society as its end, are enough for them; the brotherhood of man is no mere phrase with them, but a fact of life, and the nobility of man shines upon us from their work-hardened bodies.

MARX, from: *The Holy Family* (1845)

We come across Marie surrounded by criminals, a prostitute, a servant of the proprietress of a criminals' tavern. In this debasement she preserves a human nobleness of soul, a human unaffectedness, and a human beauty that impress those around her, raise her to the level of a poetical flower of the criminal world, and win for her the name of *Fleur de Marie.*

We must observe *Fleur de Marie* attentively from her first appearance in order to be able to compare her *original form* with her *critical transformation.**

In spite of her frailty *Fleur de Marie* shows great vitality, energy, cheerfulness, elasticity of character—qualities which alone explain her human development in her *inhuman* situation. . . .

Good and *evil*, in Marie's mind, are not the moral *abstractions* of good and evil. She is *good* because she has never caused *suffering* to anybody, she has always been *human* towards her inhuman surroundings. She is *good* because the sun and the flowers reveal to her her own sunny and blossoming nature. She is *good* because she is still *young*, full of hope and vitality. Her situation is *not good* because it does her unnatural violence, because it is not the expression of her human impulses, the fulfillment of her human desires; because it is full of torment and void of pleasure. She measures her situation in life by her *own individuality*, her *natural* essence, not by the *ideal of good*.

In *natural* surroundings the chains of bourgeois life fall off *Fleur de Marie*; she can freely manifest her own nature and consequently is bubbling with love of life, with a wealth of feeling, with human joy at the beauty of nature; these show that the bourgeois system has only grazed the surface of her and is a mere misfortune, that she herself is neither good nor bad, but *human*. . . .

So far we have seen *Fleur de Marie* in her original un-critical form. Eugène Sue has here risen above the horizon of his own narrow world outlook. He has slapped bourgeois prejudice in the face. He will hand over *Fleur de Marie* to the hero Rudolph to make up for his own rashness and to reap applause from all old men and women, from the whole of the Paris police, from the current religion and from "Critical Criticism.". . .

In her unhappy situation in life she was able to become a lovable, human individual; in her exterior debasement she was conscious that *her human* essence was *her true essence*. Now the filth of modern society which has come into exterior contact with her becomes her innermost being; continual hypochondriac self-torture because of that filth will be her duty, the task of her life appointed by God himself, the self-aim of her existence.

* Again, the novel *The Mysteries of Paris* by Sue is the reference, in which Fleur de Marie appears as a major figure. Sue and his Young Hegelian "Critical" critic Szeliga are both regarded as warping a true portrait of this human type by their speculative commentaries.

MARX, from: *Introduction to the Critique of Political Economy* (1857)

6. *The unequal relation between the development of material production and e.g., artistic production.* On the whole, the conception of progress should not be accepted in the usual abstraction. Modern art, etc. It is not as important and difficult to grasp this disproportion as that within practical social relations, e.g., the relation between education in the United States and Europe. The really difficult point to be discussed here, however, concerns how the productive relations come forward as legal relations in an unequal development. Thus, e.g., the relation between Roman civil law (this is less true of criminal and public law) and modern production.

7. *This conception of development appears to imply necessity.* On the other hand, justification of accident. Varia. (Freedom and other points.) (The effect of means of communication. World history did not always exist; history as a consequence of world history.)

8. *The starting point is of course in certain facts of nature;* subjective and objective. Clans, races, etc.

It is well known that certain periods of highest development of art stand in no direct connection with the general development of society, nor with the material basis and the skeleton structure of its organization. Witness the example of the Greeks as compared with modern art or even Shakespeare. As concerns certain forms of art, e.g., the epos, it is even acknowledged that as soon as the production of art as such appears they can never be produced in their epoch-making, classical aspect; and accordingly, that in the domain of art certain of its important forms are possible only at an undeveloped stage of art development. If that is true of the mutual relations of different modes of art within the domain of art itself, it is far less surprising that the same is true of the relations of art as a whole to the general development of society. The difficulty lies only in the general formulation of these contradictions. No sooner are they made specific than they are clarified.

Let us take for instance the relationship of Greek art and then Shakespeare's to the present. It is a well known fact that Greek mythology was not only the arsenal of Greek art but also the very ground from which it had sprung. Is the view of nature and of social relations which shaped Greek imagination and thus Greek [mythology] possible in the age of automatic machinery and railways and locomotives and electric telegraphs? Where does Vulcan come in as against Roberts & Co., Jupiter as against the lightning rod, and Hermes as against the Crédit Mobilier? All mythology masters and dominates and shapes the forces of nature in and through the imagination; hence it disappears as soon as man gains mastery over the forces of nature. What becomes of the Goddess Fame side by side with Printing House Square? Greek art presupposes the existence of Greek mythology, i.e., that nature and even the forms of society itself are worked up in the popular imagination in an unconsciously artistic fashion. That is its material. Not, however, any mythology taken at random, nor any accidental unconsciously artistic elaboration of nature (including with the latter everything objective, hence society too). Egyptian mythology could never be the soil or the womb which would give birth to Greek art. But in any event [there had to be] *a* mythology. There could be no social development which excludes all mythological relation to nature, all mythologizing relation to it, and which accordingly claims from the artist an imagination free of mythology.

Looking at it from another side: is Achilles possible where there are powder and lead? Or is the *Iliad* at all possible in a time of the hand-operated or the later steam press? Are not singing and reciting and the muse necessarily put out of existence by the printer's bar; and do not necessary prerequisites of epic poetry accordingly vanish?

But the difficulty does not lie in understanding that the Greek art and epos are bound up with certain forms of social development. It rather lies in understanding why they still afford us aesthetic enjoyment and in certain respects prevail as the standard and model beyond attainment.

A man cannot become a child again unless he becomes childish. But doesn't he enjoy the naive ways of the child, and mustn't he himself strive to reproduce its truth again at a higher stage? Isn't the character of every epoch revived perfectly true to nature in child nature? Why should the historical childhood of humanity, where it had obtained its most beautiful development, not exert an eternal charm as an age that will never return? There are ill-bred children and precocious children. Many of the ancient peoples belong to these categories. But the Greeks were normal children. The charm their art has for us does not stand in contradiction with the undeveloped stage of the social order from which it had sprung. It is much more the result of the latter, and inseparately connected with the circumstance that the unripe

135

social conditions under which the art arose and under which alone it could appear can never return.

FORM AND STYLE

ENGELS, from: Letter to Wilhelm Gräber, October 8, 1839

I devote myself at present to the modern style which, without doubt, is of all stylistics the ideal.* Its model can be found in the writings of Heine, and especially in those of Kühne and Gutzkow. Its master, however, is Wienbarg. Earlier Lessing, Goethe, Jean Paul, and above all Börne contributed elements that have had an especially favorable effect upon it. The style of Börne, ah, that surpasses all! *Menzel, der Franzosenfresser* is stylistically the best of all German works and is additionally the first one to destroy an author completely when it was important to do so. It has been banned in Germany again so that one will have to follow a mediocre style as is practiced in the royal bureaus. The modern style combines the best of all styles in itself: terse conciseness and pregnancy which hits its mark with a *single* word, alternating with epic, calm description; simple speech, alternating with scintillating images and glittering sparks of wit, a strong youthful Ganymede, roses wound round his head and the weapon in hand that slew the python. Thus, too, the individuality of the author is given greatest latitude, so that, in spite of the affinity, no one is the imitator of another. Heine writes dazzlingly, Wienbarg cheerfully warm and beaming, Gutzkow with a razor-sharp accuracy that carries, at times, a welcome beam of sunshine; Kühne writes good-heartedly and descriptively, with perhaps too much light and too little shadow; Laube imitates Heine and Goethe, too, but preposterously, since he imitates the Goethean Varnhagen, copied likewise by Mundt. Marggraf is still inclined to generalize with his cheeks full, but that will stop, and the prose of Beck has not yet gotten beyond the stage of studies.—If the ornate style of Jean Paul is united with Börne's precision, you have the basic traits of the modern style. Gutzkow was fortunate enough to know how to absorb the brilliant, nimble yet dry style of the French. This French style is like a gossamer web; the German modern is a silken flock. (This image misses

* The nineteen-year-old Engels wrote his study of style as a letter to a childhood friend. At the time he was hopeful of following in the steps of literary authors in the 'modern style.' Karl Ludwig Borne (1786-1837), Karl Gutzkow (1811-1878), Gustav Kühne (1806-1888), Heinrich Laube (1806-1884), and Theodor Mundt (1808-1861) belonged to the 'Young Germany' movement which influenced young Engels' world view. Karl August von Ense Varnhagen (1785-1858) was an eminent liberal critic, biographer and historian, friendly to this movement. Jean Paul (J.P.F. Richter, 1763-1825) was a famous Romantic writer, one of the exponents of *Romantische Ironie*.

its mark, I fear.) That I nonetheless do not ignore the old in pursuit of the new is shown by my studies of the inspired songs by Goethe. They must be studied for their musical character, which is done in compositions by various hands.

MARX, from: Letter to Frederick Engels, October 26, 1854

I have come back to the worthy Chateaubriand,* this *belletrist*, who in the most objectionable fashion combines the eighteenth century's elegant scepticism and Voltairianism with the elegant sentimentalism and romanticism of the nineteenth century. Of course, in France this combination had to prove epoch-making *stylistically*, although its artificiality even in the style hits you in the eye despite the neat artistic stratagems. As far as this fellow is concerned *politically*, he revealed himself completely in his *Congrès de Vérone* (1838) and the only question still uncertain is whether he "accepted cash" from [the Tsar of Russia] Alexander Pavlovitch, or whether this foolish fop was simply bought by flattery which he cannot at all resist. In any event, he received the Order of St. Andrew from Petersburg. The *vanitas* peeps from every pore of M. le "Vicomte" (?), despite his coquettish, sometimes Mephistophelean and sometimes Christian, continual play with the *vanitatum vanitas*. You know that at the time of the Congress [1822] Villèle was prime minister under Louis XVIII, and Chateaubriand the French emissary to Verona. In his *Congrès de Vérone*—perhaps you read it at one time—he reports on the proceedings and decisions, etc. It begins with a short history of the Spanish Revolution of 1820-23. As concerns this "history," it's enough to take note that he misplaces Madrid on the Tajo (just to bring in the Spanish saying that this river *cria oro* (hatches forth gold), and that in his recounting, Riego leading

* François-René vicomte de Chauteaubriand (1768-1848), noted French author (*Atala, Rene,* etc.), statesman and diplomat, was French foreign minister for two years after the 1822 Congress of Verona. Further comment on Chauteaubriand's style appears in a letter from Marx to Engels of November 30, 1873: "I have read Saint-Beuve's book on *Chateaubriand*, a writer who has always been repugnant to me. If the man has grown so famous in France, it is because he is the most classic incarnation of French *vanité* in every regard, and this *vanité* not in a light, frivolous eighteenth-century raiment, but priding itself on Romantic garb and the very latest turns of phrase. The false profundity, Byzantine exaggeration, emotional coquetry, play of motley iridescence, word painting, theatrical, sublime—in one word, in form and content a never-before-seen mishmash of lies."

10,000 men (in fact there were 5,000) attacked by General Freyre, who led 13,000; after his defeat, Riego then retreated with *15,000* men. He has him withdraw to the Sierra Morena rather than the Sierra de Ronda, in order to compare him with the hero of La Mancha (Don Quixote). I mention this *en passant* to characterize his manner. Scarcely any data correct.

M. Chateaubriand's deeds at the Congress of Verona provide, however, the best joke; after it ended, he became minister of foreign affairs and conducted the military invasion of Spain....

MARX, from: Letter to Ferdinand Lassalle, April 19, 1859

I come now to *Franz von Sickingen.** First I must praise the composition and the action, which is more than one can say for any other modern German drama. In the second instance, and laying aside any purely critical relation to the work, it affected me strongly on the first reading, and so, it will have an even stronger effect on readers who are more emotionally disposed. And this is a second very important aspect. Now the other side of the medal: first of all—a purely formal concern—since you have written in verse, you could haved worked on your iambics somewhat more artistically. However, irrespective of how shocking this carelessness will be to the *poets by profession*, I consider this an advantage since our spawn of poetical epigones have nothing left to offer but formal polish.

* The major portion of this letter is reproduced in the section "The Problem of Realism."

ENGELS, from: Letter to Ferdinand Lassalle, May 18, 1859

Dear Lassalle:

You are probably somewhat surprised that I have not written you for so long, especially as I owe you my opinion of *Sickingen.** But it was just this that has delayed me so long. With the drought of fine literature which now prevails everywhere, I seldom read such works, and it has been years since I last read one of them with the purpose of giving a thorough judgment, a definite substantiated opinion. The usual

* The bulk of this letter appears under the heading "The Problem of Realism."

trash is not worth it. Even the few fairly good English novels which I still read from time to time, like Thackeray's for instance, have not been able to interest me to this extent even once, although they undoubtedly have a literary and cultural-historical significance. But due to such a long lack of exercise, my critical faculties have grown dull, and I must take considerable time before I can give a definite opinion. Your *Sickingen* deserves a different attitude than those literary products, and so I did not grudge it the time. The first and second reading of your—in every sense, both as to theme and treatment—national German drama, emotionally affected me so strongly that I was compelled to put it aside for a while; the more so since my taste, crudened by these days of literary poverty, has brought me to such a state (I confess it, to my shame) that even things of slight value may at times make some impression on me at *first* reading. So, in order to achieve a wholly nonpartisan, perfectly "critical" attitude, I put *Sickingen* aside, i.e. lent it to some acquaintances (there are still a few Germans here more or less educated in literature). *Habent sua fata libelli* [books have their fate]—if you lend them, they seldom return, and so I had to obtain the return of my *Sickingen* by force. I can tell you that after a third and fourth reading my impression has remained the same, and being certain that your *Sickingen* can stand criticism, I am now going to apply the "acid test."

I know it will be no great compliment to say that not one of the official poets of Germany today is even remotely capable of writing such a drama. But it is a fact, and one too characteristic of our literature to pass by in silence. First, let me discuss the formal side. Here I must note that I was most pleasantly surprised by the skillful handling of the knots and the thoroughly dramatic character of the play. To be sure you have allowed yourself many liberties in the versification which however are more troublesome in reading than on the stage. I should have liked to read the stage adaptation; as the play stands, it certainly could not be staged. I was visited by a young German poet (Karl Siebel), a countryman and distant relative, who has worked a good deal in the theatre; as a reservist of the Prussian guard, he perhaps will be in Berlin, so I may take the liberty of having him bring you a note. He has a very high opinion of your drama, but thinks it entirely impossible to stage on account of the long monologues which provide for only one actor to do something while the others would have exhausted their supply of mimicry two and three times over not to stand there like part of the scenery. The last two acts prove that you could make the dialogue vivacious and quick without difficulty, and with the exception of several scenes (which happens in every play), this could be done in the first three acts also. So I have no doubt that in preparing your play for the stage, you will have taken this into consideration. The *intellectual content* must, of course, suffer from this, as is inevitable, and the perfect fusion of the greater intellectual depth, of conscious historical content, with which you justly credit German drama, with Shakespearian vivacity and wealth of action will probably be achieved only in the future and perhaps not by Germans. It is truly in this fusion that I see the future of the drama. Your *Sickingen* is wholly on the right track; the principal characters *are* representatives of distinct classes and tendencies and hence definite ideas of their time, and the motives of their actions are to be found not in trivial individual desires but in the historical stream upon which they are carried. However, the next step forward should be in making these motives emerge to the foreground in a more lively, active, as it were natural way from the course of action itself, on the other hand making the argumentative speeches (in which, by the way, I recognize with pleasure your old oratorical talents from the courts of justice and the popular assembly) less and less necessary. You, too, seem to recognize this as the ideal aim, while establishing the difference between a stage play and a literary play; I think *Sickingen* could, even though with difficulty (because to achieve perfection is not so simple), be made over into a stage play in this sense. The characterization of the persons is connected to this. You quite justly object to the *poor* individualization which prevails at present, which comes to nothing but clever little, excremental tid-bits and is a fundamental symptom of an epigone literature that is elapsing and vanishing. It seems to me, however, that the person is characterized not only by *what* he does but also by *how* he does it; and from this point of view, I do not think it would have harmed the intellectual content of your drama if the individual characters had been more sharply differentiated and their mutual oppositions brought out. The characteristics which sufficed in *antiquity* are no longer adequate in our age, and in this, it seems to me, you could have paid more attention to the significance of Shakespeare in the history of the development of the drama without damaging your own work. But these are secondary matters, and I only mention them so that you may see that I have also given some thought to the formal aspects of your play.

MARX, from: Letter to J.B. Schweitzer, January 24, 1865

[Proudhon's] first work, *What is Property?*, is by all means his best work. It is epoch-making, if not for the newness of its content, then at least for the new and audacious way in which old things are said....

In Proudhon's book [of 1840] there still prevails, if I may be allowed the expression, a strong muscular style. And its style is in my opinion its chief merit. One sees that even where he is only reproducing old stuff, Proudhon makes independent discoveries; that what he is saying was new to him himself and ranks as new. Provocative defiance, laying hands on the economic "holy of holies," superb paradox which makes a mock of bourgeois common sense, withering criticism, bitter irony, and, betrayed here and there, a deep and genuine feeling of indignation at the infamy of what exists, revolutionary earnestness—because of all this *What Is Property?* had an electrifying effect and made a great impression on its first appearance. In a strictly scientific history of political economy the book would hardly be worth mentioning. But sensational works of this kind play their part in the sciences just as much as in polite literature....

In *The Philosophy of Poverty* [1846] all the defects of Proudhon's method of presentation stand out very unfavorably in comparison with *What Is Property?* The style is often what the French call *ampoulé* [bombastic]. High-sounding speculative jargon, supposed to be German-philosophical, appears regularly on the scene when his Gallic acumen fails him. A puffing, self-glorifying, boastful tone, and especially the twaddle about "*science*" and the sham display of it, which are always so unedifying, continually explode in one's ears. Instead of the genuine warmth which glowed in his first piece of writing, certain passages here are systematically and rhetorically worked up into a momentary fever.

SUPPLEMENT

ELEANOR MARX, from: "Recollections of Mohr" (1895)

He was a unique, an unrivalled story-teller.* I have heard my aunts say that as a little boy he was a terrible tyrant to his sisters, whom he would "drive" down the Markusberg at Trier full speed, as his horses, and worse, would insist on their eating the "cakes" he made with dirty dough and dirtier hands. But they stood the "driving" and ate the "cakes" without a murmer, for the sake of the stories Karl would tell them as a reward for their virtue. And so many and many a year later Marx told stories to his children. To my sisters—I was then too small—he told tales as they went for walks, and these tales were measured by miles not chapters. "Tell us another mile," was the cry of the two girls. For my own part, of the many wonderful tales Mohr told me, the most wonderful, the most delightful one, was "Hans Röckle." It went on for months and months; it was a whole series of stories. The pity no one was there to write down these tales so full of poetry, of wit, of humour! Hans Röckle himself was a Hoffmann-like** magician, who kept a toyshop, and who was always "hard up." His shop was full of the most wonderful things—of wooden men and women, giants and dwarfs, kings and queens, workmen and masters, animals and birds as numerous as Noah got into the Arc, tables and chairs, carriages, boxes of all sorts and sizes. And though he was a magician, Hans could never meet his obligations either to the devil or the butcher, and was therefore—much against the grain—constantly obliged to sell his toys to the devil. These then went through wonderful adventures—always ending in a return to Hans Röckle's shop. Some of these adventures were as grim, as terrible, as any of Hoffmann's; some were comic; all were told with inexhaustible verve, wit and humour.

And Mohr would also read to his children. Thus to me, as to my sisters before me, he read the whole of Homer, the whole *Nibelungen Lied, Gudrun, Don Quixote,* the *Arabian Nights,* etc. As to Shakespeare he was the Bible of our house, seldom out of our hands or mouths. By the time I was six I knew scene upon scene of Shakespeare by heart.

On my sixth birthday Mohr presented me with my first novel —the immortal *Peter Simple.*** This was followed by a whole course of Marryat and Cooper. And my father actually read every one of the tales as I read them, and gravely discussed

* Eleanor Marx wrote the memoir of her father in English. "Mohr" was Marx's lifelong nickname.
** E.T.A. Hoffmann (1776-1822), famous romantic author.
*** *Peter Simple,* novel by Frederick Marryat (1792-1848), English novelist, seaman, author of adventure tales.

147

them with his little girl. And when that little girl, fired by Marryat's tales of the sea, declared she would become a "Post-Captain" (whatever that may be) and consulted her father as to whether it would not be possible for her "to dress up as a boy" and "run away to join a man-of-war" he assured her he thought it might very well be done, only they must say nothing about it to anyone until all plans were well matured. Before these plans could be matured, however, the Scott mania had set in, and the little girl heard to her horror that she herself partly belonged to the detested clan of Campbell. Then came plots for rousing the Highlands, and for reviving "the forty-five." I should add that Scott was an author to whom Marx again and again returned, whom he admired and knew as well as he did Balzac and Fielding. And while he talked about these and many other books he would, all unconscious though she was of it, show his little girl where to look for all that was finest and best in the works, teach her—though she never thought she was being taught, to that she would have objected—to try and think, to try and understand for herself.

And in the same way this "bitter" and "embittered" man would talk "politics" and "religion" with the little girl. How well I remember, when I was perhaps some five or six years old, feeling certain religious qualms and (we had been to a Roman Catholic Church to hear the beautiful music) confiding them, of course, to Mohr, and how he quietly made everything clear and straight, so that from that hour to this no doubt could ever cross my mind again. And how I remember his telling me the story—I do not think it could ever have been so told before or since—of the carpenter whom the rich men killed, and many and many a time saying, "After all we can forgive Christianity much, because it taught us the worship of the child."

ELEANOR MARX, Notes on the Friendship of Heine and Marx (1895)

I remember both my parents and Helen [Demuth] speaking much of Heine, whom (in the early forties) they saw constantly and intimately.* It is no exaggeration to say that Mohr not only admired Heine as a poet, but had a sincere affection for him. He would even make all sorts of excuses for Heine's political vagaries. Poets, Mohr maintained, were queer kittle-cattle, not

* This text was written in English at the request of Karl Kautsky, and has not been previously published. It appears by courtesy of the International Institute of Social History, Amsterdam.

to be judged by the ordinary, or even the extra-ordinary standards of conduct. My mother—for whose beauty and wit Heine had a profound admiration—was less lenient, and I have heard Mohr tell again and again, with infinite gusto, how Möhme (my mother) would quite ignore the fact that Heine was a great poet and rake him soundly as a very weak man.

It is an interesting fact—as I have heard my parents say—Heine used, at one time, to run up constantly to their rooms, to read them his "verses" and ask their opinion. Again and again Mohr would go over some "small thing" of eight lines, discussing, analyzing. To those who imagine immortal poems like Heine's are written without effort or travail of spirit it may be worth recalling that this great poet would come up day after day to read and re-read some poem; would discuss the superiority of this over that word; would in a word, polish his poems till every sign of labour and polish had been effaced.

One of the things Mohr found it most difficult to bear patiently was Heine's morbid susceptibility to criticism—even to the criticism of people for whom he had the profoundest contempt. He would come crying—*literally*—the tears running down his cheeks—if some wretched penny-a-liner had fallen foul of him. Then Mohr's one remedy was to send Heine to his wife. "Go and cry to Jenny" he would say—and she with her witty, caustic, albeit kindly tongue, would soon brace up the despondent poet.

One thing I have often heard from Mohr and Möhme—that whereas Herwegh** (whom my parents were very fond of) used to have his rooms arranged in the most luxurious fashion, Heine's room was that of an anchorite. Herwegh had gorgeous carpets, curtains, furniture. Heine a bare room; a table, chair, and desk.

But, the thing that after all Mohr and Mohme and our dear old Nymmy*** best remembered, was an occasion where the Poet distinctly showed himself the most practical man. My sister Jenny, then a baby some months old, was taken with some sort of fit or convulsions. Mohr, Möhme and Helen were all helpless and in despair. Heine arrived on the scene. "Put the baby in a bath" quoth the poet—and with his own hands prepared the bath, put the baby in it, and so, as Mohr said, saved Jenny's life.

** Georg Herwegh (1817-1875), a poet of 1848 and member of the early workers movement, a friend of Marx from 1842, long in exile from Germany.

*** Nymmy, or Helen Demuth, was the household helper and friend of the Marx family.

Politically, so far as I understand, they seldom discussed things. But certainly Mohr judged Heine very tenderly, and he loved not only the man's work, but also the man himself.

PAUL LAFARGUE, from: Reminiscences of Marx (1890)

He knew Heine and Goethe by heart and often quoted them in his conversations; he was an assiduous reader of poets in all European languages.* Every year he read Aeschylus in the Greek original. He considered him and Shakespeare as the greatest dramatic geniuses humanity ever gave birth to. His respect for Shakespeare was boundless: he made a detailed study of his works and knew even the least important of his characters. His whole family had a real cult for the great English dramatist; his three daughters knew many of his works by heart. When after 1848 he wanted to perfect his knowledge of English, which he could already read, he sought out and classified all Shakespeare's original expressions. He did the same with part of the polemical works of William Cobbett, of whom he had a high opinion. Dante and Robert Burns ranked among his favorite poets and he would listen with great pleasure to his daughters reciting or singing the Scottish poet's satires or ballads.

From time to time, he would lie down on the sofa and read a novel; he sometimes read two or three at a time, alternating one with another. Like Darwin, he was a great reader of novels, his preference being for those of the eighteenth century, particularly Fielding's *Tom Jones*. The more modern novelists whom he found most interesting were Paul de Kock, Charles Lever, Alexander Dumas senior and Walter Scott, whose *Old Mortality* he considered a masterpiece. He had a definite preference for stories of adventure and humor.

He ranked Cervantes and Balzac above all other novelists. In *Don Quixote* he saw the epic of dying-out chivalry whose virtues were ridiculed and scoffed at in the emerging bourgeois world. He admired Balzac so much that he wished to write a review of his great work *La Comédie Humaine* as soon as he had finished his book on economics. He considered Balzac not only as the historian of his time, but as the prophetic creator of characters which were still in the embryo in the days of Louis Philippe and did not fully develop until after his death, under Napoleon III.

* Paul Lafargue, author of this reminiscence, was a son-in-law of Karl Marx.

He had an incomparably fertile imagination: his first literary works were poems. Mrs. Marx carefully preserved the poetry her husband wrote in his youth but never showed it to anybody. His family had dreamt of him being a man of letters or a professor and thought he was debasing himself by engaging in socialist agitation and political economy, which was then disdained in Germany.

Marx had promised his daughters to write a drama on the Gracchi for them. Unfortunately he was unable to keep his word. It would have been interesting to see how he, who was called "the knight of the class struggle," would have dealt with that terrible and magnificent episode in the class struggle of the ancient world.

FRANZISKA KUGELMANN, from: "Small Traits of Marx's Great Character" (1928)

When anybody showed exaggerated feeling in his presence Marx liked to recall Heine's lines:*

Ein Fräulein stand am Meere,	[A girl stood by the seashore
Ihr war so weh und bang,	In such great pain and dread.
Es grämte sie so sehre,	What was all her grief for?
Der Sonnenuntergang.	Because the sun had set.]

Marx had known Heine and visited the unfortunate poet during his last illness in Paris. Heine's bed was being changed as Marx entered. His sufferings were so great that he could not bear to be touched, and the nurses carried him to his bed in a sheet. But Heine's wit did not forsake him and he said to Marx in a feeble voice: "See, my dear Marx, the ladies still carry me aloft."

Marx was of the opinion that all Heine's wonderful songs about love were the fruit of his imagination, that he had never had any success with the ladies and had been anything but happy in his married life. Marx thought the following lines applied perfectly to his death:

---

* Franziska Kugelmann (b. 1858), author of this memoir, was the daughter of Dr. Ludwig Kugelmann, a democrat and participant in the 1848-49 Revolution, at whose home Marx stayed while correcting proofs for the first volume of *Capital* in 1867.

Um sechse ward er gehenkt,	[At six he was executed,
Um sieben ward er ins Grab gesenkt,	At seven laid in the grave
Sie aber schon um achte	And lo! as eight was striking
Trank roten Wein und lachte.	She drank red wine in high glee.]

Marx's opinion of Heine's character was by no means a good one. In particular he accused him of ingratitude to friends who had helped him. For instance, the completely unjustifiable irony of the lines on Christiani: "For a youth so amiable no praise is too great," etc.

There was probably no field of science into which he had not penetrated deeply, no art for which he was not an enthusiast, no beauty of nature which did not arouse his admiration. But he could not bear truthlessness, hollowness, boasting or pretense.

My mother's best friend was Frau Tenge, an outstanding woman in every way, excellent in the true sense of the word. She was of the Bolongaro-Crevenna family from Frankfurt am Main. She had married the great Westphalian landholder Tenge-Rietberg, and they lived on the feudal property near Rheda. These two friends often visited one another. Frau Tenge always used the same small bedchamber at our house when she came to stay, and she called in "my room." My mother now wrote her about the interesting visitor, inviting her to come over to Hanover to make his acquaintance. Frau Tenge gladly accepted and said she could spend several days. Because Marx was occupying "her room," my mother asked him to move to another during her stay.

Marx was immensely pleased with this admirable woman, who played the piano with artistry. Wonderful days were spent together, filled with animated conversation and high good humor that remained indelibly in the memories of all of us. Marx's taste was most refined in poetry as well as in the sciences and visual arts. He was extraordinarily well-read and had a remarkable memory. He shared my father's enthusiasm for the great poets of classical Greece, Shakespeare and Goethe; Chamisso** and Rückert*** were also among his favorites. He would quote Chamisso's touching poem "The Beggar and His Dog." He admired Rückert's way with language and especially his masterly translation of Hariri's *Maqāmas*,**** so incom-

---

** Adalbert von Chamisso (1781-1838), a liberal romantic poet.
*** Friedrich Ruckert (1788-1866), a late romantic poet, most noted for his translations from Oriental literatures.
**** Abu Mohammed Kasim ibn Ali Hariri (1054-1122), Arab poet and philologist.

parably original. This was presented years later by Marx to my mother, in remembrance of that time.

Marx was remarkably gifted for languages. Besides English, he knew French so well that he himself translated *Capital* into French,***** and his knowledge of Greek, Latin, Spanish and Russian was so good that he could translate them at sight. He learned Russian by himself "as a diversion" when he was suffering from carbuncles. He was of the opinion that Turgenev wonderfully renders the peculiarities of the Russian soul in its veiled Slavonic sensitivity. Lermontov's descriptions, he thought, were hardly to be surpassed and seldom equalled. His favorite author among the Spaniards was Calderon.****** Marx had several of his works with him and often read parts aloud.

In the evening, preferably at twilight, everyone took pleasure in the splendor of Frau Tenge's piano playing. As it happened, she brought her own visitor's book to Hanover to have it rebound. This could not be done as well in little Rheda or in nearby Bielefeld as in the larger city. When the time came for her to return home, she asked Marx to write something in the book; because he had occupied her room he had, she said, actually been her guest too. Marx acceded to the wish and wrote:

La vida es sueño, un frenesie, una ilusión,
So lehrt uns Meister Calderón.
Doch zähl ich's zu den schönsten Illusionen,
Das Fremdenbuch Tenge-Crevenna zu bewohnen.

[Life is a dream, a frenzy, an illusion,
This is taught us by masterly Calderón.
Thus I count it a very beautiful illusion
To find, in the book of Tenge-Crevenna, a home.]

After Frau Tenge departed my mother accidentally found a scrap of paper on which were verses from which the above was extracted. It ran in full:

***** Marx did not translate the first volume of *Capital* into French, rather he carefully edited the translation of J. Roy, with which he was dissatisfied.
****** Pedro Calderón de la Barca (1600-1681), Spanish dramatist, whose *La Vida es Sueño* (Life is a Dream) is the best known of his 120 plays.

La vida es sueño, un frenesie, una ilusion,
So lehrt uns Meister Calderón.
Doch wenn Tonmeere Deiner Hand entschäumen,
Möcht ich für alle Ewigkeiten träumen.
Es zähmt des Lebens wilde Phrenesie
Der Zauber weiblich edler Harmonie,
Doch zähl ich's zu den schönsten Illusionen,
Das Fremdenbuch Tenge-Crevenna zu bewohnen.

[Life is a dream, a frenzy, an illusion,
This is taught us by masterly Calderón.
Yet, when your hand skims over oceans of tones,
I could dream for all of eternity.
Magically tamed is life's wild frenzy,
By a womanly noble harmony,
Thus I count it a very beautiful illusion
To find, in the book of Tenge-Crevenna, a home.]

My parents stated their great regret that only a part of these beautiful thoughts had been inscribed, but Marx responded that the complete verse would have been too much for a visitor's book....

In later years, Marx sent some books to my mother in memory of the talks together: Rückert's translation of Hariri's *Maqãmas*, Chamisso's works, and E.T.A. Hoffmann's *Klein Zaches*. This satire in the form of a legend particularly amused Marx.

BIBLIOGRAPHY

The following bibliography is a compilation of books in English which have a bearing on Marxist aesthetics. Not all books are strictly speaking Marxist, but all make an important contribution toward a historical understanding of the development of Marxist theories about literature and art. The bibliography is based to a certain extent on Lee Baxandall's Marxism and Aesthetics: A Selective Annotated Bibliography *(New York: Humanities Press, 1968), which contains references to articles and pamphlets as well. However, since his work only covers the period up till 1968, additions and corrections have been made. Wherever possible, the publisher's name has been included to help the reader locate a book more readily. We have also tried to specify revised and new editions. No attempt has been made to be comprehensive. Our main purpose has been to provide a useful listing of books which deal with questions of Marxist aesthetics. The list was compiled by staff members of* New German Critique, *David Bathrick, Tom Moylan, and Jack Zipes.*

Anthologies and Bibliographies

Aptheker, Herbert, ed. *Marxism and Alienation: A Symposium.* American Institute for Marxist Studies. Monograph Series No. 2. New York: Humanities Press, 1965.

Art and Society: A Collection of Articles. Moscow: Progress, 1968.

Baxandall, Lee. *Marxism and Aesthetics: A Selective Annotated Bibliography.* New York: Humanities Press, 1968.

————, ed. *Radical Perspectives in the Arts.* Baltimore: Penguin, 1972.

College English: Special Issue on Marxist Criticism. Vol. 34, No. 2, November, 1972. Eds. Ira Shor and Dick Wasson.

Counts, George S. and Lodge, Nucia, eds. *The Country of the Blind.* Boston, 1949.

Day-Lewis, Cecil, ed. *The Mind in Chains. Socialism and the Cultural Revolution.* London, 1937.

Delany, Sheila. *Counter-Tradition: A Reader in the Literature of Dissent and Alternatives.* New York: Basic Books, 1971.

Duncan, Hugh D. *Annotated Bibliography on the Sociology of Literature.* Chicago, 1947.

Ehrmann, Jacques, ed. *Literature and Revolution.* Boston: Beacon, 1967.

Flores, Angel, ed. *Literature and Marxism: A Controversy by Soviet Critics.* New York, 1938.

Harap, Louis. *A Brief Bibliography of Marxism and the Arts*. Marxism and Culture No. 1, issued by Educational Department, Cultural Division, Communist Party, State of New York, n.d.

Howard, Dick and Klare, Karl, eds. *The Unknown Dimension: European Marxism since Lenin*. New York: Basic Books, 1972.

Hoffman, Frederick J., Charles Allen and Carolyn F. Ulrich. *The Little Magazine: A History and a Bibliography*. Princeton: Princeton University Press, 1947.

Kampf, Louis and Lauter, Paul, eds. *The Politics of Literature: Dissenting Essays on the Teaching of English*. New York: Random House, 1970.

Kettle, Arnold, ed. *Shakespeare in a Changing World*. New York: New World Paperback, 1964.

Lachs, John. *Marxist Philosophy: A Bibliographical Guide*. Chapel Hill: University of North Carolina Press, 1967.

Lang, Berel and Williams, Forrest. *Marxism and Art*. New York: David McKay, 1972.

LeRoy, Gaylord C. and Beitz, Ursula, eds. *Preserve and Create: Essays in Marxist Literary Criticism*. New York: Humanities Press, 1973.

Mészáros, István, ed. *Aspects of History and Class Consciousness*. London: Routledge and Kegan Paul, 1971.

Mozhnyagun, Sergei, ed. *Problems of Modern Aesthetics*. Moscow: Progress, 1969.

North, Joseph, ed. *New Masses: An Anthology of the Rebel Thirties*. New York: International, 1972.

Parkinson, G.H.R., ed. *Georg Lukács*. London: Weidenfeld and Nicolson, 1970.

Samarin, Roman and Nikolyukin, Alexander, eds. *Shakespeare in the Soviet Union: A Collection of Articles*. Moscow: Progress, 1966.

Scott, H.G., ed. *Problems of Soviet Literature*. Moscow, 1935.

Silber, Irwin, ed. *Voices of National Liberation*. Brooklyn: Central Book, 1970.

Socialist Realism in Literature and Art. Moscow: Progress, 1971.

Solomon, Maynard. *Marxism and Art*. New York: Knopf, 1973.

Suvin, Darko, ed. *Other Worlds, Other Seas: Science Fiction from the Socialist Countries*. New York: Random House, 1970.

The Philosophical Forum: Special Issue on Georg Lukács. Boston: Boston University Press.

Tri-Quarterly: Special Issue on Literature and Revolution. No. 23/24, Winter/Spring, 1972.

White, George Abbott and Newman, Charles, eds. *Literature in Revolution.* New York: Holt, Rinehart, and Winston, 1972.

Women and Art: Special Issue on Marxism and Art. Winter, 1971.

Individual Works

Aaron, Daniel. *Writers on the Left.* New York: Avon, 1965.

Adereth, M. *Commitment in Modern French Literature.* New York: Schocken, 1968.

Adorno, Theodor and Eisler, Hanns. *Composing for the Films.* New York, 1947.

Adorno, Theodor. *Prisms.* London: Neville Spearman, 1967.

————. *Philosophy of Modern Music.* New York: Seabury Press, 1971.

————. *Negative Dialectic.* New York: Seabury Press, 1972.

————. *The Jargon of Authenticity.* Evanston: Northwestern University Press, 1973.

Althusser, Louis. *Lenin and Philosophy and Other Essays.* New York: Monthly Review Press, 1972.

Antal, Frederick. *Florentine Painting and its Social Background: XIV and Early XV Centuries.* London: Kegan Paul, 1948.

————. *Fuseli Studies.* London: Kegan Paul, 1956.

————. *Hogarth and his Place in European Art.* New York: Basic Books, 1962.

————. *Classicism and Romanticism.* London: Kegan Paul, 1966.

Apresyan, Z. *Freedom and the Artist.* Moscow: Progress, 1968.

Aron, Raymond. *Marxism and the Existentialists.* New York: Harper and Row, 1969.

Auerbach, Erich. *Mimesis.* Princeton: Princeton University Press, 1970.

Bakhtin, Mikhail. *Rabelais and His World.* Cambridge: M.I.T. University Press, 1968.

Balázs, Béla. *Theory of the Film: Character and Growth of a New Art.* London: Peter Smith, 1952; New York: Dover, 1970; rev. ed. New York: British Book Center, 1971.

Baller, E. *Socialism and the Cultural Heritage.* Moscow: Novosti Publishers, 1968.

Barthes, Roland. *Critical Essays.* Evanston: Northwestern University Press, 1972.

————. *Mythologies*. New York: Hill and Wang, 1972.

————. *On Racine*. New York: Hill and Wang, 1964.

————. *Writing Degree Zero and Elements of Semiology*. Boston: Beacon, 1970.

Benjamin, Walter. *Illuminations*. New York: Schocken, 1966.

————. *Understanding Brecht*. London: New Left Books, 1973.

————. *Charles Baudelaire: A Lyric Poet in the Era of High Capitalism*. London: New Left Books, 1973.

Berger, John. *Art and Revolution*. New York: Pantheon, 1969.

————. *Moment of Cubism*. New York: Pantheon, 1969.

————. *Toward Reality: Essays in Seeing*. New York: Knopf, 1962.

————. *A Painter of Our Time*. New York: Simon and Schuster, 1959.

————. *Success and Failure of Picasso*. Baltimore: Penguin, 1965.

Blake, Fay M. *The Strike in the American Novel*. Metuchen, N.J.: Scarecrow Press, 1972.

Bloch, Ernst. *Philosophy of the Future*. New York: Herder and Herder, 1970.

————. *Man on His Own: Essays in the Philosophy of Religion*. New York: Herder and Herder, 1971.

————. *On Karl Marx*. New York: Herder and Herder, 1971.

————. *The Spirit of Utopia*. New York: Seabury Press, 1973.

Blumenfeld, Y. *Seesaw: Cultural Life in Eastern Europe*. New York: Harcourt, 1968.

Bramsted, Ernest K. *Aristocracy and the Middle Classes in Germany: Social Types in German Literature 1830-1900*. Rev. ed. Chicago: University of Chicago Press, 1964.

Brecht, Bertolt. *Brecht on Theatre*. ed. John Willett. New York: Hill and Wang, 1964.

————. *The Messingkauf Dialogues*. London: Methuen, 1965.

Breton, André. *What Is Surrealism?* London: Criterion Miscellany, 1936; also in *Paths to the Present*, ed. Eugene Weber. New York: Dodd, Mead, 1960.

————. *Manifestoes of Surrealism*. Ann Arbor: University of Michigan Press, 1969.

Bronowski, Jacob. *William Blake: A Man Without a Mask*. London, 1944.

Browder, Earl. *Communism and Culture*. New York, 1941.

Bukharin, Nikolai. *Historical Materialism: A System of Sociology*. New York, 1925; London: Russell and Russell, 1965.

————. *Culture in Two Worlds*. New York, 1934.

Burgum, E.B. *The Novel and the World's Dilemma*. New York: Oxford University Press, 1947.

Castro, Fidel. *The Revolution and Cultural Problems in Cuba.* Havana, 1962.

Calverton, Victor F. *The Newer Spirit: A Sociological Criticism of Literature.* New York, 1925; New York: Octagon Press, 1972.

———. *The Liberation of American Literature.* New York, 1932; New York: Octagon Press, 1972.

———. *Where Angels Fear to Tread.* facs. ed. Freeport, N.Y.: Books for Libraries, 1941.

Caudwell, Christopher. *Studies and Further Studies in a Dying Culture.* New York: Monthly Review Press, 1972; originally published as *Studies in a Dying Culture.* London, 1938; *Further Studies in a Dying Culture.* London, 1949.

———. *The Concept of Freedom.* London: Lawrence and Wishart, 1965.

———. *Romance and Realism: A Study in English Bourgeois Literature.* Princeton: Princeton University Press, 1970.

———. *Illusion and Reality: A Study of the Sources of Poetry.* London, 1937; New York: New World Paperback, 1963.

Caute, David. *Communism and the French Intellectuals, 1914-1960.* New York: Macmillan, 1964.

———. *The Fellow Travellers: A Postscript to the Enlightenment.* New York: Macmillan, 1972.

———. *The Illusion: An Essay on Politics, Theater, and the Novel.* New York: Harper and Row, 1971.

Ching, Chiang. *On the Revolution of the Peking Opera.* Peking: Foreign Language Press, 1968.

Cruse, Harold. *The Crisis of the Negro Intellectual.* New York: Morrow, 1967.

Davydov, Yuri. *The October Revolution and the Arts.* Moscow: Progress, 1967.

Day-Lewis, Cecil. *A Hope for Poetry.* London, 1934.

———. *Revolution in Writing.* London, 1935.

Delany, Sheila. *Chaucer's House of Fame: The Poetics of Skeptical Fideism.* Chicago: University of Chicago Press, 1972.

Deutscher, Isaac. *Heretics and Renegades.* London, 1955; New York: Bobbs-Merrill, 1969.

———. *Ironies of History: Essays on Contemporary Communism.* New York: Oxford University Press, 1966; San Francisco: Ramparts Press, 1971.

———. *Marxism in Our Time.* San Francisco: Ramparts Press, 1971.

Egbert, D.D. *Socialism and American Art: In the Light of European Utopianism, Marxism, and Anarchism.* Princeton:

Princeton University Press, 1952. Paperback, 1967.

———. *Social Radicalism and the Arts: Western Europe.* New York: Knopf, 1970.

———, Stow Pearsons and T.D. Seymour Bassett, eds. *Socialism and American Life,* 2 vols. Princeton: Princeton University Press, 1952.

Ehrenburg, Ilya. *Chekov, Stendhal and Other Essays.* London: MacGibbon and Kee, 1961.

Eisenstein, Sergi. *Notes of a Film Director.* Moscow: Foreign Languages Publishing House, 1946.

———. *Film Form and Film Sense.* New York: Meridian, 1957; also published separately, *Film Form.* New York: Harcourt, Brace, Jovanovich, 1969. *Film Sense.* New York: Harcourt, Brace, Jovanovich, 1969.

———. *Film Essays and a Lecture.* New York: Praeger, 1970.

Ewen, Frederic. *Bertolt Brecht: His Life, His Art and His Times.* New York: Citadel, 1967.

Fan, L.H., ed. *The Chinese Cultural Revolution: Selected Documents.* New York: Grove Press, 1968.

Farrell, James T. *A Note on Literary Criticism.* New York: Vanguard, 1936.

———. *Literature and Morality.* 1947.

———. *Reflections at Fifty.* New York: Vanguard, 1954.

Fast, Howard. *Literature and Reality.* New York, 1950.

———. *The Naked God: The Writer and the Communist Party.* New York, 1957.

Finkelstein, Sidney. *Art and Society.* New York: International, 1947.

———. *Jazz: A People's Music.* New York, 1948.

———. *How Music Expresses Ideas.* New York: International, 1952; rev. ed. 1970.

———. *Realism in Art.* New York: International, 1954.

———. *Composer and Nation: The Folk Heritage of Music.* New York: International, 1960.

———. *Existentialism and Alienation in American Literature.* New York: International, 1965.

———. *Sense and Nonsense of McLuhan.* New York: International, 1968.

———. *Who Needs Shakespeare?* New York: International, 1973.

Fischer, Ernst. *The Necessity of Art.* London: Pelican, 1963.

———. *Art Against Ideology.* New York: Braziller, 1969.

Fitzpatrick, Sheila. *The Commissariat of Enlightenment: Soviet Organization of Education and the Arts under Lunacharsky, October 1917-1921.* Cambridge: Cambridge University Press,

1970.

Fokkema, D.W. *Literary Doctrine in China and Soviet Influence, 1956-1960.* The Hague: Mouton, 1965.

Fox, Ralph. *Aspects of Dialectical Materialism.* London, 1934.

———. *The Novel and the People.* London, 1937; New York: International, 1945.

Garaudy, Roger. *Literature of the Graveyard.* New York, 1948.

———. *Marxism in the Twentieth Century.* New York: Scribner, 1970.

———. *Crisis in Communism.* New York: Grove Press, 1972.

Gilbert, James B. *Writers and Partisans: A History of Literary Radicalism in America.* New York: John Wiley, 1968.

Gold, Mike. *Mike Gold: A Literary Anthology.* ed. M. Folsom. New York: International, 1972.

Goldmann, Lucien. *The Hidden God.* New York: Humanities Press, 1964; London: Routledge and Kegan, 1964.

———. *The Human Sciences and Philosophy.* London: Jonathan Cape, 1969; New York: Grossman, 1969.

———. *Immanuel Kant.* New York: Humanities Press, 1972.

Goldman, Merle. *Literary Dissent in Communist China.* Cambridge: Harvard University Press, 1967.

Gorky, Maxim. *Fragments from My Diary.* London: P. Allan, 1924.

———. *Culture and the People.* Freeport, New York: Books for Libraries, facs. ed., 1939.

———. *Creative Labour and Culture.* Sidney, 1945.

———. *Literature and Life.* London, 1946.

———. *On Literature.* Moscow: Foreign Language Publishing House, 1960; Seattle: University of Washington Press, 1968.

———. *The Autobiography of Maxim Gorky.* New York: Macmillan, 1962; London: Peter Smith.

———. *Untimely Thoughts: Essays on Revolution, Culture and the Bolsheviks, 1917-18.* New York: Paul Eriksson, 1968.

———. *Reminiscences.* New York: Humanities Press, 1968; New York: Viking Press, 1973.

Gramsci, Antonio. *Modern Prince and Other Writings.* London, 1957; New York: International, 1969.

———. *Prison Notebooks.* London, 1970; New York: International, 1971.

Hauser, Arnold. *The Social History of Art.* New York: Knopf, 1951; 4 vols. New York: Vintage, 1957.

———. *The Philosophy of Art History.* New York: Knopf, 1958.

———. *Mannerism: The Crisis of the Renaissance and the Origin of Modern Art.* 2 vols. New York: Knopf, 1965.

Henderson, Philip. *Literature and a Changing Civilization.* London, 1935; Folcroft, Pa.: Folcroft Press, 1935.

―――. *The Novel Today: Studies in Contemporary Attitudes.* London, 1936; Folcroft, Pa.: Folcroft Press, 1936.

―――. *Poet and Society.* London, 1939; Folcroft, Pa.: Folcroft Press, 1939.

―――. *William Morris: His Life, Work, and Friends.* New York: McGraw-Hill, 1967.

―――. *Marlowe.* New York: British Book Center, 1967.

Hoggart, Richard. *Auden: An Introductory Essay.* New York: Hillary Press, 1965.

―――. *The Uses of Literacy: Aspects of Working Class Life.* London: 1957; New York: Oxford University Press, 1957; Boston: Beacon 1961; New York: Oxford University Press, 1970.

―――. *Speaking to Each Other: Vol. 1, About Society; Vol. 2, About Literature.* New York: Oxford University Press, 1970.

―――. *On Culture and Communication.* New York: Oxford University Press, 1972.

Horkheimer, Max. *Critical Theory.* New York: Herder and Herder, 1972.

Horkheimer, Max and Adorno, Theodor. *Dialectic of Enlightenment.* New York: Herder and Herder, 1972; London: Penguin, 1973.

Jackson, T.A. *Dialectics: The Logic of Marxism and Its Critics.* New York: International, 1936; New York: B. Franklin, 1971.

―――. *Charles Dickens: The Progress of a Radical.* London, 1937; New York: International, 1938; New York: Haskell, 1971.

―――. *Old Friends to Keep: Studies of English Novels and Novelists.* London, 1950.

James, C.L.R. *The Old World and the New: Shakespeare, Melville, and Others.* Detroit: Facing Reality Publications, 1971.

Jameson, Fredric. *Marxism and Form: Twentieth Century Dialectical Theories of Literature.* Princeton: Princeton University Press, 1972.

―――. *The Prison House of Language: A Critical Account of Structuralism and Russian Formalism.* Princeton: Princeton University Press, 1972.

Jarvie, Ian C. *Toward a Sociology of the Cinema.* London, 1970.

Jerome, V.J. *Culture in a Changing World.* New York, 1947.

Kautsky, Karl. *Thomas More and his Utopia.* New York, 1927; New York: Russell and Russell, 1959.

―――. *Foundations of Christianity.* New York, 1953.

Kettle, Arnold. *Introduction to the English Novel.* 2 vols. London: Hutchinson, 1955; New York: Harper and Row, 1960.

―――. *Communism and the Intellectuals.* London: Lawrence and Wishart, 1965.

Khrushchev, Nikita. *The Great Mission of Literature and Art.* Moscow, 1964.

Klingender, Francis D., ed. *Hogarth and English Caricature.* London, 1944.

―――. *Marxism and Modern Art.* New York: International, 1945.

―――. *Goya in the Democratic Tradition.* London, 1948; New York: Schocken, 1968.

―――. *Art and the Industrial Revolution.* London, 1947; East Orange, N.J.: Thomas Kelly, 1968.

―――. *Animals in Art and Thought to the End of the Middle Ages.* Cambridge, Mass.: M.I.T. Press, 1971.

Knight, Frida. *Beethoven.* New York: International, 1973.

Konrad, N.I. *West-East: Inseparable Twain.* Moscow: Central Department of Oriental Literature, 1967.

Kott, Jan. *Shakespeare Our Contemporary.* New York: Doubleday, 1964.

―――. *The Eating of the Gods: An Interpretation of Greek Tragedy.* New York: Random House, 1973.

Kozintsev, Grigori. *Shakespeare.* New York: Hill and Wang, 1966.

Labriola, Antonio. *Socialism and Philosophy.* Chicago, 1907.

―――. *Essays on the Materialistic Conception of History.* Chicago, 1908.

Lafargue, Paul. *Social and Philosophical Studies.* Chicago, 1906.

―――. *The Right to Be Lazy and Other Studies.* Chicago, 1909; New York: Solidarity, 1969.

―――. *Origin and Evolution of the Idea of the Soul.* Chicago, 1922.

―――. *Socialism and the Intellectuals.* New York: Labor News, 1967.

Lang, Ian. *Jazz in Perspective: The Background of the Blues.* London: Workers Music Association, 1947.

Larkin, Oliver. *Art and Life in America.* New York, 1949.

Lawson, John Howard. *Film: The Creative Process.* New York: 1964.

Lenin, V.I. *On Tolstoy.* Moscow: Foreign Languages Publishing House, 1950.

―――. *On Culture and Cultural Revolution.* Moscow: Progress, 1966.

————. *On Literature and Art.* Moscow: Progress, 1967.

LeRoy, Gaylord. *Marxism and Modern Literature.* American Institute for Marxist Studies. No. 5. New York: Humanities Press, 1967.

Leger, Fernand. *Functions of Painting.* New York: Viking, 1973.

Leyda, Jay. *Kino: A History of the Russian and Soviet Film.* New York, 1960.

Lifschitz, Mikhail. *The Philosophy of Art of Karl Marx.* New York, 1938.

Lindsay, Jack. *After the Thirties: The Novel in Britain and its Future.* London, 1956.

————. *The Anatomy of Spirit.* London, 1937.

————. *John Bunyan: Maker of Myths.* London, 1937; Clifton, N.J.: Augustus M. Kelley, 1937; Port Washington, N.Y.: Kennikat Press, 1969.

————. *Perspectives for Poetry.* London, 1944.

————. *Song of a Falling World: Culture During the Break-up of the Roman Empire, A.D. 350-600.* London: Dakars, 1948.

————. *Marxism and Contemporary Science.* London: D. Dobson, 1949.

————. *Charles Dickens.* London, 1950; New York: Philosophical Library, 1950.

————. *A World Ahead.* London, 1950.

————. *Byzantium into Europe.* London, 1952; New York: Humanities Press, 1952.

————. *George Meredith, His Life and Works.* London, 1956.

————, ed. *Russian Poetry 1917-1955.* Bodley Head: London, 1957.

————. *Death of the Hero: French Painting from David to Delacroix.* London: Studio, 1960.

————. *William Morris, Writer.* London, 1971.

————. *A Short History of Culture: From Prehistory to the Renaissance.* New York: Citadel, 1963.

————. *Leisure and Pleasure in Roman Egypt.* London: Muller, 1965.

————. *The Clashing Rocks: A Study of Early Greek Religion and Culture and the Origins of Drama.* London, 1965.

————. *J.M.W. Turner: A Critical Biography.* New York; New York Graphic Society, 1966.

————. *Meetings with Poets,* London: Muller, 1968.

————. *Cézanne, His Life and Art.* Greenwich: New York Graphic Society, 1968.

Lowenthal, Leo. *Literature and the Image of Man: Sociological Studies of the European Drama and Novel, 1600-1900.*

Boston: Beacon, 1957.

Lu Hsun. *Selected Works*. Peking, 1957-60.

——. *A Brief History of Chinese Fiction*. Peking, 1959.

Lukács, Georg. *Studies in European Realism*. London: Merlin, 1950; New York: Grosset and Dunlap, 1964.

——. *The Historical Novel*. London: Merlin Press, 1962; Boston: Beacon Press, 1963; New York: Humanities Press, 1965; Middlesex: Penguin, 1969.

——. *Thomas Mann*. London: Merlin Press, 1964; also available as *Essays on Thomas Mann*. New York: Grosset and Dunlap, 1965.

——. *The Meaning of Contemporary Realism*. London: Merlin, 1962; also published as *Realism in Our Time*. New York: Harper and Row, 1964.

——. *Goethe and his Age*. London: Merlin, 1968; New York: Grosset and Dunlap, 1969.

——. *The Theory of the Novel*. Cambridge: M.I.T. Press, 1971.

——. *Writer and Critic*. New York: Grosset and Dunlap, 1971.

——. *Solzhenitsyn*. Cambridge: M.I.T. Press, 1971.

——. *Marxism and Human Liberation*. New York: Dell, 1973.

Lunacharsky, Anatoli V. *On Literature and Art*. Moscow: Progress, 1965.

MacDiarmid, Hugh. *Selected Essays*. Berkeley: University of California Press, 1970.

Maguire, Robert A. *Red Virgin Soil: Soviet Literature in the 1920s*. Princeton: Princeton University Press, 1968.

Mao Tse-Tung. *On Literature and Art*. Peking: Foreign Languages Press, 1960.

Marcuse, Herbert. *Eros and Civilization*. Boston: Beacon, 1955.

——. *Soviet Marxism*. New York: Columbia University Press, 1958.

——. *Reason and Revolution: Hegel and the Rise of Social Theory*. Boston: Beacon, 1960.

——. *One-Dimensional Man*. Boston: Beacon, 1964.

——. *Negations: Essays in Critical Theory*. Boston: Beacon, 1969.

——. *An Essay on Liberation*. Boston: Beacon, 1969.

——. *Five Lectures*. Boston: Beacon, 1970.

——. *The Philosophy of Aesthetics*. New York: Humanities Press, 1972.

——. *Counterrevolution and Revolt*. Boston: Beacon, 1972.

Margolies, David. *The Function of Literature*. New York: International, 1969.

Matlaw, Ralph E., ed. *Belinsky, Chernyshevsky, and Dobrolyubor: Selected Criticism*. New York: Dutton, 1962.

Mayakovsky. Vladimir. *How Are Verses Made?* London: Jonathan Cape, 1970.

Mayer, Hans. *Steppenwolf and Everyman: Outsiders and Conformists in Contemporary Literature*. New York: Thomas Y. Crowell, 1971.

————. *Portrait of Wagner: An Illustrated Biography*. New York: Herder and Herder, 1972.

Mehring, Franz. *Karl Marx: The Story of his Life*. London: Allen, 1936; New York: Humanities Press, 1957; Ann Arbor: University of Michigan Press, 1962.

————. *The Lessing Legend*. abridged version, New York, 1938.

Meyerhold, Vsevelod. *On Theatre*. New York: Hill and Wang, 1969.

Morris, William. *On Art and Socialism: Essays and Lectures*. London, 1947.

————. *Selected Writings and Designs*. ed. Asa Briggs. Baltimore: Penguin Books, 1962.

————. *Political Writings*. New York: International, 1973.

Morton, A.L. *The English Utopia*. London, 1952.

————. *The Everlasting Gospel? A Study in the Sources of William Blake*. London, 1958.

Piscator, Erwin. *Political Theatre 1920-1966*. London: Arts Council of Great Britain, 1971.

Plekhanov, Georgi. *Anarchism and Socialism*. Chicago, 1912.

————. *Essays in the History of Materialism*. London, 1934.

————. *History of Russian Social Thought*. New York: Howard Fertig, 1938.

————. *Art and Social Life*. London: Lawrence and Wishart, 1953.

————. *Unaddressed Letters. Art and Social Life*. Moscow, 1957.

———— *Fundamental Problems of Marxism*. New York: International, 1969.

Prusek, Jaroslav. *Chinese History and Literature: A Collection of Studies*. New York: Humanities Press, 1970.

Raphael, Max. *Prehistoric Cave Paintings*. New York, 1945.

————. *Prehistoric Pottery and Civilizaton in Egypt*. New York, 1947.

————. *The Demands of Art*. Princeton: Princeton University Press, 1968.

Raskin, Jonah. *The Mythology of Imperialism*. New York: Random House, 1971.

Read, Herbert. *Phases of English Poetry*. Folcroft, Pa.: Folcroft Press, 1928.

————. *Sense of Glory: Essays in Criticism*. Facs. ed.; Freeport, N.Y.: Books for Libraries, 1930.

————. *Form in Modern Poetry*. Folcroft, Pa.: Folcroft Press, 1932.

————. *Art and Industry: The Principles of Industrial Design*. London: Peter Smith, 1934; rev. ed. Bloomington: Indiana University Press, 1961.

————. *Art and Society*. London, 1936; rev. ed. New York: Schocken, 1968.

————. *In Defense of Shelley and Other Essays*. Facs. ed.; Freeport, N.Y.: Books for Libraries, 1936.

————. *Poetry and Anarchism*. London, 1938; Folcroft, Pa.: Folcroft Press, 1938; New York: Gordon Press.

————. *Nature of Literature*. Freeport, N.Y.: Books for Libraries, 1938.

————. *The Politics of the Unpolitical*. London, 1943.

————. *Coleridge as Critic*. New York: Haskell, 1949.

————. *Wordsworth*. New York: Hillary, 1949.

————. *Philosophy of Modern Art*. Facs. Ed.; Freeport, N.Y.: Books for Libraries, 1950.

————. *Icon and Idea: The Function of Art in the Development of Human Consciousness*. London: Faber, 1955; New York: Schocken, 1965.

————. *The Grass Roots of Art: Lectures on the Social Aspects of Art in the Industrial Age*. London: Faber, 1955; New York: World, 1961.

————. *Forms of Things Unknown*. London: Faber, 1960.

————. *Art of Sculpture*. Princeton, N.J., 1961.

————. *To Hell with Culture and Other Essays on Art and Society*. New York: Schocken, 1962.

————. *Concise History of Modern Sculpture*. New York: Praeger, 1964.

————. *Contemporary British Art*. Santa Fe: William Gannon, 1964; rev. ed. Middlesex: Penguin Books, 1965.

————. *The Origins of Form in Art*. New York: Horizon, 1965.

————. *Henry Moore*. New York: Praeger, 1966.

————. *Poetry and Experience*. New York: Horizon Press, 1967.

————. *Concise History of Modern Painting*. New York: Praeger, 1969.

————. *Cult of Sincerity*. New York: Horizon Press, 1969.

————. *Art and Alienation: The Role of the Artist in Society*. New York: Vintage, 1969.

————. *Anarchy and Order*. London: Faber, 1954; Boston: Beacon Press, 1971.

————. *Reason and Romanticism*. New York: Haskell, 1972.

Revai, Josef. *Literature and People's Democracy*. New York, 1950.

Richmond, Kenneth. *Poetry and the People*. London, 1947.

Rubinstein, Annette T. *The Great Tradition in English Literature: From Shakespeare to Shaw*. New York, 1953; First half reissued as *Shakespeare to Jane Austen*. New York: Citadel, 1962.

Sartre, Jean-Paul. *Saint Genet, Actor and Martyr*. New York: Braziller, 1963.

———. *Search for a Method*. New York: Knopf, 1963.

———. *Situations*. New York: Braziller, 1965.

———. *What Is Literature?* New York: Washington Square Paperback, 1966.

Schlauch, Margaret. *Chaucer's Constance and Accused Queens*. New York: AMS Press, 1927; Staten Island: Gordian, 1970.

———. *Gift of Languages*. New York: Dover, 1942. London: Peter Smith.

———. *Modern English and American Poetry: Techniques and Ideologies*. London: C.A. Watts, 1956.

———. *English Medieval Literature and Its Social Foundations*. New York: Oxford University Press, 1956; New York: Cooper Square, 1971.

———. *Antecedents of the English Novel: 1400-1600*. London: Oxford University Press, 1963.

———. *The English Language in Modern Times (Since 1400)*. Warsaw, 1959; 2nd ed. New York: Oxford University Press, 1964.

———. *Language and the Study of Languages Today*. New York: Oxford University Press, 1967.

Schwarz, Boris. *Music and Musical Life in Soviet Life, 1917-1970*. New York: Norton, 1972.

Siegel, Paul N. *Shakespearean Tragedy and the Elizabethan Compromise*. New York: New York University Press, 1957.

———. *Shakespeare in his Time and Ours*. South Bend: University of Notre Dame Press, 1968.

Siegmeister, Elie. *Music and Society*. New York, 1938.

Sinyavsky, Andrei. *For Freedom and Imagination*. New York: Holt, Rinehart and Winston, 1971.

Slochower, Harry. *Three Ways of Modern Man*. New York: 1937.

———. *Thomas Mann's Joseph Story: An Interpretation*. New York, 1938.

———. *No Voice Is Wholly Lost*. New York, 1945; reissued as *Literature and Philosophy Between Two Wars*. New York, 1964.

———. *Mythopoesis*. Detroit, 1970.

Smirnov, A.A. *Shakespeare: A Marxist Interpretation.* New York, 1936.

Southall, Raymond. *Literature and the Rise of Capitalism.* London: Lawrence and Wishart, 1973.

Spender, Stephen. *The Destructive Element.* London, 1935; West Orange, N.J.: Saifer, 1970.

———. *Forward from Liberalism.* 1937.

———. *Life and the Poet.* London, 1942.

Stalin, Joseph. *Marxism and Linguistics.* New York, 1951.

Strachey, John. *Literature and Dialectical Materialism.* London, 1934.

———. *The Coming Struggle for Power.* London, 1935.

———. *End of Empire.* New York: Praeger, 1964.

Thomson, George. *Aeschylus and Athens: A Study in the Social Origins of Drama.* London, 1941; New York: Grossett and Dunlap, 1969.

———. *Studies in Ancient Greek Society: The Prehistoric Aegean.* London: Lawrence and Wishart, 1949; 3rd ed. New York: Citadel, 1965.

———. *Marxism and Poetry.* New York: International, 1946.

———. *Studies in Ancient Greek Society: The First Philosophers.* London: Lawrence and Wishart, 1955.

———. *Greek Lyric Meter.* Cambridge: Cambridge University Press, 1961.

Trotsky, Leon. *Literature and Revolution.* New York: Russell and Russell, 1957; Ann Arbor: University of Michigan Press, 1960.

———. *On Literature and Art.* New York: Pathfinder Press, 1970.

Van Ghent, Dorothy. *The English Novel: Form and Function.* New York, 1961.

Vygotsky, Lev. *The Psychology of Art.* Cambridge: M.I.T. Press, 1970.

Werth, Alexander. *Musical Uproar in Moscow.* London, 1949.

West, Alick. *Crisis and Criticism.* London: Lawrence and Wishart, 1937.

———. *A Good Man Fallen Among Fabians.* London, 1950.

———. *The Mountain in the Sunlight.* London, 1958.

Williams, Raymond. *Culture and Society.* London: Chatto and Windus, 1958.

———. *Modern Tragedy.* London: Chatto and Windus, 1966.

———. *The English Novel from Dickens to Lawrence.* London: Chatto and Windus, 1970.

Wilson, Edmund. *The Wound and the Bow: Seven Studies in Literature.* New York: Galaxy, 1941.

————. *The Triple Thinkers.* New York: Oxford University Press, 1948.

————. *A Literary Chronicle: 1920-1950.* New York: Doubleday Anchor, 1952.

————. *To the Finland Station: A Study in the Writing and Acting of History.* New York: Doubleday, 1953.

————. *Axel's Castle: A Study in the Imaginative Literature of 1870-1930.* New York: Scribner, 1961.

————. *The Shores of Light: A Literary Chronicle of the Twenties and Thirties.* New York: Vintage, 1961.

Zelinsky, Kornely. *Soviet Literature.* Moscow: Progress, 1970.

Zhdanov, A.A. *Essays on Literature, Philosophy and Music.* New York, 1950.